What the Pros are Saying about

"Moving from a good writer to a g
careful editing. This book gives yc
sentence structure, narrative drive, logical organization, and reader
perspective. After reading it, your writing will have professional polish."

Dennis E. Hensley, Ph.D.
author, *Finding Success with Your Dream Writing Projects*

"If you want to impress an editor, you need to edit your manuscripts
before submitting them. Linda Taylor guides you through the editing
process to create clean copy that is more likely to result in a check
instead of a rejection letter."

Lin Johnson
managing editor, *Christian Communicator*
director, Write-to-Publish Conference

"Linda Taylor has worked with major publishers and is now teaching
students at Taylor University the art and science of editing. I highly
recommend this book as an essential guide for authors in transforming
their manuscript into publishable form."

James N. Watkins
author of *Communicate to Change Lives* and *Writing*
with Banana Peels

word by word

Dear Terry —
Thanks for your
support across the years!

your friend in publishing '

Linda Taylor
July 2018

word by word

An Editor Guides Writers in the Self-Editing Process

Linda K. Taylor, MA, MFA

Bold Vision Books
PO Box 2011
Friendswood, Texas 77549

Dedication

For my grandkids

Ariadne, Alea, Micah, Damien, and Elijah.

May you come to love words as much as I do.

Table of Contents

Acknowledgments

So many people come to mind when I consider the folks who helped me learn and practice the craft. Thanks to Dr. Leax, one of my professors at Houghton College, who ignited the spark in me of understanding the joy and power of words. My first job at ETTA (now ETA) with Bob and Barb who taught me proofreader marks and the whole book publishing process. I'm thankful for a long (and continuing) career at Livingstone/Barton-Veerman Company with Bruce Barton and Dave Veerman who have trusted me with hundreds of projects, and my co-workers and fellow editors Betsy Schmitt, Linda Washington, Claudia Gerwin, and Mary Horner Collins— we hammered out systems and learned our craft (and laughed a lot).

Thanks to Dr. Dennis Hensley at Taylor University who saw a spark in me and helped me now have a job where I can pass along what I know to a new generation of writers and editors. I also thank my intrepid future writers and editors in my "From Manuscript to Book: How It Happens" class, who gamely took on their professor's book and put me through my paces. And thanks to the members of my writers group, Writers Bloc, who thoroughly yet kindly gave me feedback.

And of course, I thank my family—my husband Tom; daughter and son-in-law Courtney and Dave Jorgensen; son and daughter-in-law Tom and Jami Taylor; and son, Sean. My family watched and encouraged me over the years as I became immersed in editing and publishing books as a career. They continue to do so every day. I am humbled and honored to have them in my life.

And thanks to George and Karen Porter at Bold Vision Books for giving me this opportunity to join their stellar lineup of authors. And, of course, thank you to the patient editors who whipped this book into shape.

Introduction

You've just completed your manuscript. You put that last period in place at the end of that stunning final line. You sniff away a trickling tear. You can't believe you did it.

Congratulations!

Give yourself a nice break. Go enjoy that favorite treat. Go do that task you promised yourself you'd do "as soon as the book is finished."

You're celebrating, but in the back of your mind is that niggling thought, *I know I'm not really finished.*

That's correct. You're not finished. Getting that first draft completed is a *huge* endeavor, and you certainly deserve to celebrate. But hard work still lies ahead. Your manuscript isn't ready to submit to an editor or agent. Not yet. Rarely is anyone's first draft perfect (sorry). Now, you must dive into the process of self-editing—going back through your manuscript, asking the hard questions, digging into the tough but needed changes, and cutting and revising and rewriting.

"But how do I do that? Where do I begin?" you may be asking.

That's why I wrote this book. I'll walk you through that self-editing process.

But relax and take joy in this moment when the monumental task of writing that first draft is behind you.

In fact, I would advise you to take a real break from the manuscript—such as a few weeks. Put it away. Don't look at it. It will be simmering in your mind. To be able to effectively self-edit, however, you need a few weeks away from your work to help you see it with fresh eyes. You'll be amazed what you see that eluded you during the writing process.

While you let your manuscript simmer, let's talk about what you'll be doing when you begin to self-edit.

First, I will show you how to reconsider your first pages and determine if your beginning is your best beginning. Will these pages capture your audience? Will an editor or agent sit up and take notice? Be brutal, because these first pages are what will get you past publishing's gatekeepers. If those first readers want to keep reading, they are more apt to give your manuscript another look. It is vital to polish your beginning until it sparkles.

Next, we will examine your entire manuscript from a big-picture perspective (acting as content editors) and ask the vital questions about how the entire book holds together. If your book is fiction, how strong are your characters, dialog, settings, and pacing? If your book is nonfiction, how specific and consistent is your tone and structure? Does the book serve your target audience? I will give you guidance regarding the questions to ask of your manuscript and how to deal with the answers.

After we make the big-picture revisions, I will show you how to move on to copyediting—looking at every point of punctuation, every word, every sentence. I will include basic grammar advice, help with permissions and sourcing, and guidance for formatting your document so it will meet the standards agents or editors desire. Then, we'll proofread so your final manuscript is pristine.

Since many of you use Scripture in your writing, my final chapter will discuss how to work with Bible text in your writing.

Along the way, I will introduce you to a couple of my editorial heroes—Maxwell Perkins and Therese von Hohoff. Their stories fascinate me. Even F. Scott Fitzgerald and Harper Lee needed the guidance of good editors. These authors' willingness to allow their editors to ask the tough questions of their manuscripts and then to go back and revise those manuscripts is what turned *The Great Gatsby* and *To Kill a Mockingbird* into masterpieces.

I've been excited to write this book for you.

Years ago, as a young bespeckled girl, I decided to spend my life immersed in other people's words, finding joy and fulfillment in a job some might consider boring but to me was endlessly exciting. I've spent three decades in the world of book publishing, beginning in a small publishing company with my electric typewriter, correction tape, and not a clue about how to be an editor. I learned on the job. Now, I teach about publishing to Professional Writing students at Taylor University in Indiana, and I still manage projects and edit as a freelancer.

This book pulls together what I know and what I can pass on to help writers such as you. In my heart, I believe that we writers have a gift from God and a responsibility to put our words into the world. We also have a responsibility to the craft, to God, and to the quality of our work. We want to write good, God-honoring books.

It is to that end that I entrust this book to you. I want to help you be the best writer you can be with a clean, polished manuscript to send into the world. I hope this books helps.

1
Peeking into a Publishing House

You have big dreams for your book. You can see it, can't you? That beautiful cover emblazoned with your name. The solid feel of it in your hands. That "new book" smell that only writers and readers understand.

I want to help get you there—to that real, live, *bona fide* book! The self-editing process described in the coming chapters will strengthen your craft and help move you toward your dream of publication. You want to put your best work into the world.

You may wonder why self-editing matters so much … after all, isn't that what the editors at the publishing houses are for?

That's partially true. However, many hands touch a manuscript as it moves through a publishing house, and publishing houses are always working on tight deadlines. To provide some context, let me briefly introduce you to the book publishing process and the people involved. I hope this gives you understanding as to why delivering a solid and clean manuscript helps you and your future editors, and ultimately, helps your book be its best.

The Process of Getting Published

I assume that you're reading this book and editing your manuscript because you hope to get it published. To do so, you need to have it ready to show to an agent or acquisitions editor—and by *ready* I mean formatted correctly, edited and copyedited and proofread, with your first few pages representing your best work.

Let's jump ahead. You're meeting with an acquisitions editor from your favorite publishing house at a writers conference. You're feeling a little sweaty under the armpits. Those moments as she reads your first pages and scans through your proposal (while you sit awkwardly staring at the floor) seem to last a lifetime. You hope you remembered to put on your deodorant that morning. You also wonder why you drank so many cups of coffee during the break.

Then she says those blessed words, "This is wonderful. I'd like to see more."

Hallelujah!

You're so excited you can barely contain yourself. You walk out of the meeting room wondering if what happened actually happened or if you're going to wake up drooling on your mousepad with a blank computer page and cursor blinking at you …

When an agent or acquisitions editor responds positively to your proposal and manuscript, it is indeed an amazing feeling! And this is why you want to do so much hard work *now*—self-editing the manuscript so that it will be ready when you hear those words. Why? I can't tell you how many agents and acquisitions editors have complained that many times they request manuscripts from people and then *never receive them!* My only guess as to why this occurs is that, while the author may have polished and polished the first pages, he hasn't done the hard work required on the rest of the manuscript, or he only has those first pages and is afraid to finish the book.

Let's not allow this to happen to you. Instead, *your* manuscript is ready. Let's watch it move through the publishing process.

The People in the Book Publishing Process

Acquisitions editor

Let's say the *acquisitions editor* (AE) showed interest in your book. Don't celebrate too much yet. The manuscript still has some hurdles to jump. Just because the AE showed interest doesn't yet mean the book is under contract for publication.

During this preliminary process, the AE will want further information from you about the full book—much of this will be in your proposal. For instance, the target audience (men? women? children?

What's the difference between an agent and an acquisitions editor?

An *acquisitions editor* (AE) works for a particular publishing house. The AE is acquiring books that his publishing house is currently seeking to fill out their genre lines. Thus, while the AE may like your book, if his publisher currently has no need to acquire any more books for the fantasy line for the next couple of years, your fantasy book will be turned down. (Remember that publishers are usually acquiring a couple years in advance—it takes that long to get a book through the entire process.) Or if your book doesn't match some of the requirements of that publishing house (say, if you're in Christian publishing, theological issues might come up), then that might cause your book to be rejected. The AE will not receive payment for acquiring your book beyond his or her salary at the publishing house. In addition, sometimes the AE is also the content editor of the book; thus, he may continue working with you in the editorial process.

An *agent* works for a literary agency. The agent will mention on a website the types of books she wants to acquire. She may focus on certain genres. If an agent likes your book, she will shop it around to the various publishers with whom she has connections. If one publisher turns her down, she can go to another. She knows publishers and probably has a special relationship with some of them—what they want, what they're looking for and need right away—and she can help you shape your book to fit. An agent doesn't get paid anything up front; instead, she gets paid upon acceptance of your book (generally 15 percent of your advance and 15 percent of all royalty payments if the book sells enough to make royalties). She also will help you through the contract negotiations.

age range?), the book's tone (humor? tongue in cheek? reference?), and its length (word count helps the AE consider placement and cost calculation). The AE needs to know your background, your expertise, your passion for the project, and your all-important platform. She needs to know where your book fits both in her publishing house and in the area of this topic or genre at large.

Publishing board

She needs as much information as she can get because she next needs to "sell" your book idea to the *pub board* (publishing board).

On a set day at the publishing house, the pub board meets to discuss the various books brought back from the AEs in their visits to writers conferences (or books sent to them by agents). The members on this board vary. The *chief executive officer* (CEO) may be there acting as the keeper of the ethos of the publishing house. Does the book fit with the mission statement? Does it fit into the kind of books the house publishes? In denominational publishing, theological bent matters when considering manuscripts.

The *chief financial officer* (CFO) may be on the pub board, looking at the numbers (after all, if books don't make money, that puts the publishing house in jeopardy). He is calculating the costs: Will the book need any special treatments (for example, will it feature color pictures throughout? Or need one of those center sections of glossy paper with photos? That will affect the cost of the printing and paper). How much is the advance to the author (if any), and what is the royalty rate? How many books will be in the first print run? What should be the selling price? A *pro forma* helps to then determine if and how the book can make money for the publishing house (and for you).

The pub board may also include several salespeople—the Amazon person, the big-box store person, the independent bookstore person. But they all have the same question—especially with unknown authors. What kind of platform does the author have? What is the key selling point for this book? What genre is it and where would it be shelved in a bookstore?

Let's say your book sails through the pub board. They've sent you a contract. You've finalized your manuscript (incorporating any comments from your acquisitions editor) and sent it to the content editor who has been assigned to your book.

Content editor

The AE may or may not also be the content editor. The *content (or developmental) editor* looks at the big picture and helps to shape the book. Sometimes chapter 3 should be chapter 1. Sometimes the pacing is off. Sometimes a character seems flat. The content editor will ask good questions and offer solid advice. Keep in mind, however, that this is a conversation. You and your editor will go back and forth about the questions and how to solve any problems.

Copy editor

After you and the editor think the manuscript is solid at the big-picture level, the manuscript will move on to a *copy editor*. The copy editor reads closely for sentence construction—dangling modifiers, run-ons, and inconsistencies. The copy editor fact checks and queries if something doesn't make sense, if a transition is needed, if a character's way of speaking doesn't sound real based on your description ("Would he really say this in this way?"). He reads for clarity, queries as needed, makes the manuscript follow house style guidelines, and generally tries to make the manuscript readable and clean. The copy editor makes sure the front matter (title page, copyright page, table of contents, dedication page, etc.) and back matter (appendix, index, endnotes) are in place.

Designer

While all of this editing is happening, over in the art department, a *designer* is creating interior and cover designs. The designer needs to know trim size and page count (page count affects the size of the spine he must design), whether or not there are photos (and if they are black and white or color), and the target audience and tone. The designer creates a template (often in InDesign) into which the typesetter will flow the Word document manuscript. Then, of course, he prepares the all-important cover design—the front cover (with title, subtitle, author, and artwork), spine (with title, author, and publisher's logo), and the back cover (with synopsis, endorsements, brief author bio, and bar code with ISBN).

Typesetter

After the copy editor finalizes the manuscript, it moves to the *typesetter* who flows the Word document into the book's interior design template. The typesetter needs to know the page count (so he can make the words fit the required number of pages), whether all the chapters must start on recto (right) pages or if they can also start verso (left), what is to be in the running heads, and if the book begins at page 1 or has roman numerals in the front matter. If there are photos, he'll need to have those (in separate files such as gif or bmp) and know where to place them. He lays out the pages to avoid widows and orphans (single words or short lines standing alone at the top or bottom of a page). He then sends the PDF of the book to the proofreader.

Proofreader

The *proofreader* works on the PDF of the typeset pages, which look exactly as the book will appear in printed form. The proofreader checks the table of contents to make sure the titles and page numbers are correct, checks all the folios (page numbers) and running heads, checks the look of each page—marking widows and orphans. Only after reviewing the look of each page does the proofreader go back and, from the first page (the title page, the copyright page, the table of contents—*every* page), read *every* word. Random errors can appear even in a clean manuscript when the document is flowed into the typesetting program (a hidden tab in a Word document can suddenly rear its ugly head and space words far apart when typeset).

At this point, the publisher might hire an *indexer* if needed. Indexers usually work in tandem with the proofreaders. Indexers also need to work with PDFs because they need to place the actual and correct page numbers on the entries in the index.

The proofreader marks any needed changes on the PDF and sends them back to the typesetter to correct. After as many cross-checks as needed until the book is "perfect," the publisher sends the final PDF to the printer.

Printer

The *printer* prints the books and the covers, creates the final books, and delivers them back to the publishing house.

Getting Yourself There

Many folks will be touching, thinking about, and making decisions regarding your book once you've handed it off to a publishing house. It will be prodded and poked. It will be covered with red markings and highlights and comments. But that's all good. This is how your book will become the best it can be. Trust the process.

In this book, I want to help you self-edit as much as possible *before* you turn in that manuscript, *before* the agent or AE or editor sees it. I want to help you do the necessary cleanup (the general annoyances

I see all the time) so that your manuscript not only sparkles but is a joy for those folks to read. Then, it is more likely to be picked up by an agent or AE. Even the best idea, if it shows up on a messy manuscript, will be seen as not worth their effort. However, those newbie authors with good ideas who also show that they've done their homework, completed careful self-editing, and formatted the manuscript correctly—well, those are the authors that agents and AEs are willing to take a chance on.

Will they still poke and prod and cover it with red? You bet. It's their *job*. But if you've revised, edited, copyedited, and proofread first, you'll make their job easier. They'll be able to focus on fine tuning instead of having to do triage.

Let's get your manuscript ready for prime time.

2
Polishing the First Pages

always begin the first day of the semester in my editing class by asking my students a question.

"So tell me, what *is* editing?" It can be difficult to articulate, so I want to understand where they're at.

"It's looking for mistakes."

"What kinds of mistakes?" I ask.

"Spelling, punctuation, grammar … ."

"Okay, that's correct for some forms of copyediting and proofreading, but what about editing?"

Blank stares.

I'm assuming that, like my students, you may think that all you have to do to self-edit is read your manuscript and look for misspelled words. That's part of the process, but certainly not all of it. Your process needs to mirror what happens in a publishing house, so let's begin at the beginning.

Make a Good First Impression

Remember our scenario of you meeting with the AE at the writers conference? Remember that she only scanned the first few pages of your manuscript after hearing your pitch and looking over your proposal? If you have been studying the craft of writing, you know how important it is to grab your reader right away—from the first pages, if not the first paragraphs. You want to surprise your reader with a fresh voice, great writing, and intrigue. In the first few pages, you create a space, a world, and you invite the reader to take the journey with you.

Remember that agents and AEs are extremely busy people. Most of them have piles of manuscripts to read, plus their involvement in other manuscripts at other levels of the sales or editing process. They don't have the time to take a leisurely read of your whole manuscript and get to the "good part" in chapter 3. You must grab them in the first few pages, hook them, and make them *have* to keep reading.

The first questions you must ask after reading the first few paragraphs of your work in progress (WIP) is, "Do I want to keep reading? Am I intrigued? Do I want to find out more?" These questions apply to both fiction and nonfiction. Getting honest answers to these questions is why it helps to have other people read your work—obviously, it is difficult to answer these questions for yourself. *You're* interested (or you wouldn't have written the book), but are *your readers* interested? Only other readers can respond to whether you have hooked them.

You must be honest about this answer—and you must allow your readers to be honest. After all, if they try to be nice and not hurt your feelings, you'll show the manuscript to an agent or AE who won't worry about being quite so nice. Let's get to the truth now and fix any problems ahead of time.

If your first few pages aren't engaging, look for some that are. It might be that your excellent beginning is a few pages later in the manuscript. As you read the first pages of your manuscript, look for the following:

In fiction: In the first pages, introduce your hero, establish the world of your story, set up the tone, show the stakes or set up the conflict, establish the hero's desires, and then start the clock running to keep the reader turning pages.

In nonfiction: As in fiction, the first few pages of a nonfiction book also need to deliver—whether it's about houseplants or wombats or overcoming grief. Does it feel fascinating right from the start? Do you have an authentic voice or a new perspective on this topic that makes it different from anything else written about it? Does that authentic voice and fresh perspective come through in these first pages? Do you give your readers a clear map for where you are taking them in this book—what they will learn, what's in it for them?

In both cases: The formatting should be correct and free of grammar and punctuation mistakes. I can't stress enough that the mechanics have to be perfect in these beginning pages. That's part of making them shine. An agent or AE won't wade through poor writing for the promise of a good idea. Also, since you know the whole book, ask yourself if you keep the promises that you make in your first pages.

Other considerations:

- ✔ Does the book begin with a scene? If so, have you effectively placed your readers there so they can see it, feel it, hear it, smell it?

- ✔ Is something suspenseful or chilling happening? If so, does it come across as effective or cheesy?

- ✔ Does whatever is happening seem clichéd or overdone (à la, "It was a dark and stormy night …")?

- ✔ Do the sentences pull you along, or do you feel that you're working hard to keep reading?

- ✔ Are the sentences varied in length and structure?

Pay attention to what's going on in your gut. Be honest with yourself. That's doesn't mean that someone else will necessarily agree (that's another way that other readers and critique groups can be helpful), but consider your internal reaction.

The Value of Other Readers

I honestly believe that this kind of big-picture reading—especially of reactions to your first pages—is difficult for you to do on your manuscript. You are too close to the work. You see the story in your head, but you may have failed to give a few of those details to your readers. It takes someone else to read, get confused, and express that to you. Then you say, "Oh my! I didn't realize that was unclear!"

Most writers, such as those in a critique group, know how to write well, or at least are great readers who understand what needs to happen to improve a manuscript. Writers usually can spot where the pacing is slowing down or why a character is coming across as flat, and often can give some sound advice.

That doesn't mean that you should only show your manuscript to other writers—after all, when you're published, your readers will mostly be readers, not writers. But these first readers, these best readers, these ones who will help you get past the publishing gatekeepers, are most helpful when they can not only see the problem but also help you with a solution.

While we're discussing this, I want to put in a plug for critique groups. Having several other writers read your WIP can bring in new perspectives. That doesn't mean that all the opinions should have the same weight or that you have to incorporate every suggestion. You can't edit by committee, but it can be helpful to get a variety of opinions. These other readers can alert you to places where your manuscript needs help. In addition, you're drawing upon a pool of people with varied interests and random sets of information in their heads.

Of course, when you show your material to other writers, you'll end up with a plethora of information—and some of it may outright disagree. One person may like your beginning, while someone else doesn't. In the end, it will be up to you to sort through the responses and figure out what makes the most sense for your work. The book is yours. Feedback is essential, but so is sorting through the feedback to discern where to make adjustments. Make sure your readers are brutally honest about the beginning. Ask them where they think you're taking them. Make sure that what they think is happening is indeed where you're going in your book. Make sure that what they visualize is what you meant for them to see.

Agents and AEs want something new and fresh. They want to see vast amounts of potential in the first few pages. So take the time to get this part right.

Now let's dig into the rest of your manuscript.

3
Content Editing:
Looking at the Big Picture

Self-editing is difficult, I know. But don't be one of those writers who has piles of unfinished or unedited or unrevised manuscripts gathering dust or overflowing file drawers. If you want to get to the next step and ultimately see publication, you must do the hard work of revising and revising and revising (yes, you'll do it more than once).

At the point where we are now—the first draft written and the first few pages revised and polished—we'll begin the self-editing process. Well, we will shortly ...

I know—you want to just *be done!* Maybe your eyes glaze over every time you reread your manuscript. Maybe you're tired of it. I'll give you this advice again: Let your manuscript sit for a couple of weeks before you begin self-editing. Separate yourself from your text. Put it away (several days, a week, several weeks if possible). Stephen King has been known to put a manuscript in a drawer for several months before coming back to it with fresh eyes. You may not have that luxury (or patience), but do let it rest for a bit. The book will be waiting when you return.

Getting in the Right Frame of Mind

Writers need to accept that their manuscripts need editing—sometimes large amounts of editing. The more that you are able to do ahead of time with self-editing and peer editing, the better the manuscript will be when it reaches the hands of an agent or AE or lands on the desk of the content editor at the publishing house. If you think like an editor, you'll ask your manuscript the good questions that an editor will ask. You'll be well prepared to answer the structure questions, the point-of-view questions, the voice questions. You'll have strong reasons for why you did what you did, and you'll be able to articulate them. Every editor loves it when an author clearly shows care about the words, shows that he or she did hard work getting to the point of publishing, and is willing to consider questions and suggestions.

In an article titled "Why We All Need a Developmental Editor," Kent Hall puts it this way: "Writers often struggle with keeping perspective on their own work; they're too close to it to know what does or doesn't work for another reader. Writers unconsciously fill in the narrative gaps with their own knowledge of the book. They can be enthralled with their subject, without considering general interest. This lack of perspective can apply to fiction and non-fiction writers."[1]

This is why other readers (such as in a critique group) are vital in this editing process—from studying the first pages to reading the entire manuscript. Think about it. You have lived in your fictional world for months, maybe years. You know exactly how the house looks and can visualize the view across the landscape. You can see the fine features and rugged attire of your protagonist. It's *there* for you. But how well did you translate that information to the page? Do your readers see what you see?

I've sat in on many a critique group where we read a piece and then someone asked, referring to the protagonist, "How old is this person?" The author was surprised that we didn't know—because he knows how old the character is and exactly how he looks. But if readers aren't told in some way (it doesn't have to be a number; sometimes grey hair or arthritic hands or loving 1940s Doo-Wop music can be enough of a clue to the character's age), then they won't be able to see what you see.

Another way critique groups and other readers can be invaluable is by offering advice or spot checking facts throughout your manuscript. A group of readers will have a wide range of interests and knowledge. For instance, a few months ago, my critique group was brainstorming some ways to kill a person and make it untraceable. This was to be part of one of our member's Amish novels. We live near Amish country, so the author has a good understanding of her setting and characters, but she needed some help with a way to commit the murder using what would be available on an Amish farm and would be untraceable. Her initial idea got some pushback from one of our members who had been a chemistry major in college and noticed that what she was suggesting simply wouldn't work chemically. The discussion about various fluids that might be available to an Amish farmer and could kill just with fumes ... well, let's just say it was fascinating.

Or consider your nonfiction manuscript. You've got a level of expertise in the topic, but you may assume way too much initial knowledge on the part of your readers. Your critique group can point out words that are too technical and therefore unclear, they can tell you if you're off in the weeds giving explanations that aren't important for the readers to know, or they can tell you if your memoir is getting off track or making the timeline difficult to follow.

I recall reading a friend's memoir WIP and asking, "Wait! I thought you said you had a brother and a sister. Who, then, is this person?" She responded with surprise. She then realized that she hadn't introduced this new character—her other sister—properly.

Let me clarify, however. Don't try to do this kind of self-editing while you're writing your first draft. It takes different "eyes" to edit than it does to write. Writing and editing are different processes and take different mind-sets. Obviously, you'll have nothing to edit if you haven't written. But if you obsessively edit and edit and re-read and re-read, revise and revise, you won't ever finish.

Being Your Own Content Editor

With all this talk of critique groups and other readers, you may wonder if it's even possible to content edit your manuscript. It is indeed difficult because you're so close to your work, but you can do a certain amount of big-picture self-editing.

Keep track of the big picture

Just as you have to not try to content edit while you write, you also have to be careful not to copyedit while you content edit. Keep

Every time I show my manuscript to my critique group, I get different opinions and don't know what to do.

As you listen to their critiques, take notes. You do want to give real credence to everyone's comments. Then, after your critique session when you're ready to work on your manuscript, pull out the list and go through it. Some people's comments may have more weight than others simply based on what you know of those people—their personalities, experience, and the tenor of the advice you've heard them give others (some people have pet peeves that they may zero in on with all manuscripts). It could be that one reader was confused about something because he didn't read thoroughly or carefully.

Listen to your gut. If something is confusing to several of your readers, take a second look and deal with that. If someone suggested rearranging chapters, consider it and see if it will improve or confuse. You only need to take the advice you feel will improve your manuscript.

the content editing phase separate from the copyediting phase, which will come next. That is, don't obsess over spelling or punctuation or rewrite sentences while you're reading for pace and plot and structure. That can become frustrating as it switches your focus back and forth and you'll lose track of what you're doing. (Trust me on this. I'm trying to keep you sane.)

Thus, as you go through the manuscript at the big-picture phase, if you read something that's unclear or awkward, mark it in red or highlight it, and keep going. You'll focus on those fixes later.

Focus your theme

What is the overarching theme of your book, and can you articulate it in one sentence? The theme isn't what the book is *about;* instead, the theme is the universal truth of your book, the comment on the human condition, the meaning behind the story. While your story is set in a particular place at a particular time with specific characters, to make it relatable and readable, hang it on a theme. The theme draws in your readers (and, incidentally, this one sentence that encapsulates your theme will serve you well as you write your proposal and pitch your book). Focusing on the theme will also help you in the revision process because it will focus your writing.

For example, let's say your fantasy story has its own world and characters with magical powers. But your overarching theme focuses on the power of family to help us be the best we can be. Knowing that this is your theme helps you stay focused—it might show that you need to get rid of a certain ancillary character; it might help you delete stray scenes that aren't advancing the story.

But one caveat: Don't let your theme run away with you. If you try to write just to the theme, you'll sound preachy. If you're too focused on "the power of family," you might not create the complex characters in that family—for instance, those great people should be allowed to make mistakes. No one is perfect, and a perfect character is flat and boring and unrelatable.

Without a theme, your writing comes across as just reporting. However, focusing too much on the theme as you write can cause everything to lead to a foregone conclusion, which makes for lazy (and boring) writing. But letting your draft guide you to a theme (you might have discovered a new or separate theme as you wrote), and then editing with that theme in mind will help you stay laser focused.

Picture your audience

Full disclosure: This is difficult for me. In fact, the first draft of this book was completely cut apart, revised, and rewritten (with many sections deleted). Why? Because my editor read it and told me I was all over the place—my audience was unclear. And she was right. Sometimes I was writing this as a textbook for my students; sometimes I was writing to the person who already has a manuscript at a publishing house and is working with an editor; sometimes I was writing to people who are critiquing others' manuscripts; sometimes I was writing to people who want to become editors. Only sometimes was I writing to the true audience of this book—the person who has a first draft written and knows that self-editing is next but doesn't know where to begin.

When I pictured *that* person, then the entire revision process became much more focused (it wasn't necessarily easier—*ouch*, it hurt to cut some of my brilliant writing!). But I knew the book would be better for it.

Picture your audience—one person to whom you're writing. Writing to that person affects your voice, your tone, even your vocabulary. Then, as you edit, consider if you're writing to that person or if you're off in the weeds somewhere.

Manage the details

Know what type of narrator you've chosen to be (first person, third person, omniscient?) and edit to see if you're consistent. For example, if you're a first-person-limited narrator, then don't veer off into sharing the thoughts of another character because you couldn't know that information.

You also need to edit for point of view (POV). Do you stay in a consistent POV, or do you jump from character's head to character's head? If your chosen POV allows you to jump around, have you included scene breaks (extra space between sections) to help the reader stay oriented? Can your readers follow which head they're in at any given time?

Print it!

I know ... that manuscript you hold in your hands already feels perfect. It looks good. But that's the problem when we type our nice neat lines on our black and white pages on our computer screens. It *looks* good. And all you can see is that window on your screen as the words scroll on by. But you need to mix it up.

As you self-edit at this big-picture phase, look for structural issues. In order to see the book's structure, it helps to see your pages differently. Print the pages and work on hard copy. In all my years of editing, I'm always amazed how different the words look on hard copy versus on a screen. Print the manuscript and lay the pages (perhaps a chapter at a time) on the floor. The printed pages help you visually see long blocks of text or other possible problems. As I was self-editing this book, I laid the pages of each chapter across my living room floor.

I could see where I had big blocks of text that needed to be broken up with subheads, as well as places that had subheads too close together.

Fiction writer and instructor William Haywood Henderson, whom I sat under in my MFA studies at Ashland University, discusses the importance of understanding the revision process. He separates "revising" and "editing," and I think he has a point. I want to step back one more segment from even the big-picture view and ask you to reread your manuscript with new eyes. Think about the following, as suggested by Henderson:

> The terms "revise" and "edit" are often used inter-changeably. ... To "revise" means "to look again," and when we talk about doing a major revision, we're talking about seeing your work with fresh eyes, taking it apart, putting it back together in a different order, cutting away excess material, altering plot points and character motivations, breaking the spine of the story, and on and on. You end up with a draft that is substantially different, page by page, but also *more purely about what the story's about on every page.*[2]

And you thought you were almost finished ...

But this revision, this going back to critique your manuscript from a big-picture perspective, is vital. If you don't do it, the editor will. And if you do it, and you still have an editor wanting to make large-scale changes, you will at least have thought through the possibilities and be able to push back a little (because you already considered what the editor is suggesting and here's why you don't want to do it) or the clouds will suddenly part and that editor is suggesting exactly that last piece your book needs—the answer to that niggling problem.

Henderson goes on:

> Revision isn't about answering questions. Revision is about breaking the perfect surface of your story, finding the questions that should have been asked, scaring yourself, reaching for strangeness and beauty, creating something wholly new and tight and wonderful from

the material your subconscious handed to you. You're finding the true story. You're digging down to the story that only you can tell. ... You have to return to your project after exposing it to the harsh light of day. This is where true revision takes over. You aren't looking for places to make things clearer (editing), you're looking for places to break things open and make the story more wonderful, complex, meaningful. There's no pussyfooting around in revision."[3]

Use some kind of system to "take apart" your manuscript. If you're writing nonfiction, you might pull out a stack of index cards and capture every segment of your book, every anecdote, every example as it stands currently. In fiction, take note of every scene, every entrance of a character and bit of information learned about that character at that point in the story. Henderson calls this segmentation "breaking the surface" of your story.

You might need to create a detailed revised outline. As part of her feedback on the first draft of this book, my editor told me to do just that. I balked a little at first. *Why do I need an outline at this point in the process?* I wondered. I didn't want to do it. Then I decided I should do it since she had asked me to do it. And she was the editor ...

I'm so thankful I did.

I read my manuscript again, looking at every paragraph or section. I wrote up my outline and plugged each piece where it belonged—*if* it belonged—and revised the outline as I went along. I questioned whether each section spoke to the target audience and to the focus of this book. I broke up a large chapter. I deleted whole sections. I discovered holes I needed to fill. Then, I took my scissors after the hard copy, moving cut-up sections into piles representing my new, focused chapters. Those piles of paper guided me as I revised the electronic manuscript.

Print your manuscript and take the scissors to it. Cut apart the various scenes or segments. Play with whether some part might work better somewhere else. This system is completely non-threatening because you're not messing with anything in your actual document yet. See if this breaking-apart process reveals to you any holes you still need to fill, any redundancies, any problems in the flow.

Questions to Ask When Content Editing Fiction

When you're self-editing your fiction manuscript, be on the lookout for (and ask your readers to be on the lookout for) the answers to several questions.

Plot arc

- ✔ Have you constructed a clear, convincing, and compelling story? (Again, what happens in your gut as you read?) Is there an arc of conflict, crisis, and resolution?

- ✔ Are you getting bored in certain spots? Mark these for later revision.

- ✔ Does the narrative flow, or do you feel confused?

- ✔ Does the resolution feel authentic and satisfying, or does it feel contrived?

- ✔ Are all of the plot lines resolved, or is anything left hanging?

- ✔ Does the pacing feel right, or does the action slow down in some places? Mark these for later revision.

- ✔ Is the story appropriate for where you hope to get published? (Certain types of storylines will be more acceptable at some Christian publishers and not others, some secular publishers and not others.)

Characters

- ✔ Have you created believable, memorable, complex characters—like real people? Or are they caricatures or stereotypes?

- ✔ Do you like or dislike the characters—or are they flat and you don't feel anything at all about them?

✔ Is the dialog vivid and realistic? Do the characters have unique voices?

✔ Are the characters developed in various ways—through description, dialogue, and actions?

✔ Are you *telling* or *showing*?

✔ Is the POV consistent? If you jump around into different people's heads, does the reader follow where you are at all times?

Setting

✔ Do you feel immersed in the book's world? Can you see it? Hear it? Smell it? Taste it? Feel it?

✔ If it's a real historical or geographical setting, is it sufficiently and accurately developed?

✔ Does the setting enhance the story—almost like it's its own character?

✔ Are the details vivid? Do they go together to make a believable world?

Questions to Ask When Content Editing Nonfiction

Note: Remember that nonfiction can encompass many different types of writing—from your basic how-to books to a creative nonfiction memoir that is full of characters and dialog and setting. Thus, some questions that you ask of fiction also apply to some types of nonfiction. Be sure to consider these as you begin your editing process of your nonfiction work.

Topic

✔ Whatever the topic, do you feel that you have focused on your audience and made it interesting to them?

✔ How did you teach about this topic to your audience? Do you feel you were successful?

✔ If this topic is replete with its own language (such as the sciences or medicine or computers), were you careful to explain terms that need definition but not be overly technical for your audience?

✔ Did you consider your audience's needs? What's in it for them? Is this clearly spelled out so your audience knows what they're getting? Is it clear how they will benefit from reading the book? Do you keep your promise of those benefits?

Logic and flow

✔ Is the content organized?

✔ Does the manuscript flow logically?

✔ If the book is topic driven, are the subheads helpful? And if there aren't any, should there be? Would they help the reader?

✔ If the book is a memoir, autobiography, or biography, are the storyline and timeline clear and easy to follow?

Audience

✔ Is it clear who the audience is?

✔ Do the writing style, vocabulary, tone, and language match the audience you want to reach?

Bible knowledge and theological issues

✔ Clear handling of Scripture is important in Christian publishing. Many Christian publishers are tied to denominations, so are you aware of their theology and pitching the book to a publisher that will not take issue with that theology?

✔ If the nonfiction book quotes the Bible or uses Bible stories, are you quoting the Bible in context and using God's Word correctly?

✔ Is there too much Christianese? We Christians have our own vocabulary and lingo. If the book is meant for a wider audience, realize that nonbelievers may not understand our buzz words—salvation, sanctification, etc.

Questions to Ask When Content Editing Both Fiction and Nonfiction

Theme(s)

✔ What theme (or themes, there can be more than one) do you desire to communicate?

✔ Is the theme preachy and overdone, or is it subtle enough to be satisfying?

✔ If there is symbolism or the use of images throughout the book, do they reflect the theme?

✔ Does the theme arise naturally out of the characters or the plot, or does it seem forced?

Passion

✔ Does the passion you have for this topic come through in your writing?

✔ Do you feel you accomplished what you promised your readers by the end—what you wanted them to know, feel, understand, or do?

Mechanics and writing quality

✔ While mechanics and writing quality should not be your focus while reading as a content editor, if you are getting distracted by errors in spelling, grammar, and punctuation, then the agent or AE will also. Don't correct them during your big-picture editing phase. Circle them to fix later, and stay focused on the big picture.

✔ Is there a lot of passive voice (if you start to notice it, then there's too much)

✔ Do you rely too much on –*ly* adverbs? Revise to find stronger verbs and more impactful words.

✔ Is every word the best word?

✔ Do the sentence lengths and structures vary?

✔ Does the prose flow and sing? Are the sentences lyrical and enjoyable, or does it feel like plodding?

The Impact of Two Great Editors

When you ask the right questions of your work, when you're willing to go back and shed the tears over massive revisions—even wholesale changes like POV or narrative structure—you might just create a masterpiece. That's what happened when two editors worked on two works that have become American classics.

Tay Hohoff

Most folks don't know the name Tay Hohoff, but if not for her, the world might never have been treated to Harper Lee's *To Kill a Mockingbird*. Certainly, Harper Lee had writing talent, but the nurturing and guidance of a top-notch editor took what began (and the world now knows) as the manuscript for *Go Set a Watchman* and helped shepherd it into a classic work with over 40 million copies sold.

The original manuscript, titled *Atticus,* arrived at J. B. Lippincott

Publishers in 1957. Therese von Hohoff, born in 1899 and at the time a 57-year-old editor at Lippincott, sat in an editorial meeting in the company's offices on Fifth Avenue in New York City one hot June day. She and Nelle Harper Lee were the only women in a sea of suits.

But apparently, that wasn't a problem for the formidable Hohoff, who went by the name Tay. She may have had grey hair pulled into a tight bun, been short, thin, addicted to cigarettes, and dealing with failing eyesight, but at Lippincott, she was a force to be reckoned with. She had joined the publishing house in 1942 and by the 1970s rose to become senior vice president—at the time a rare role for a woman.

But in that 1957 meeting, as the suited editors sat around the big table, Harper Lee probably felt like a deer in the headlights. The editorial team at Lippincott liked the manuscript and the characters but pointed out structural problems—such as how the series of anecdotes didn't hang together as a fully conceived novel. Lee listened to the nuggets of wisdom given by these veteran editors and promised to do her best as she went back to revise her manuscript.

Anyone who has ever sat in a meeting where people attempt to edit by committee know that the result usually is a muddled mess. If left to her own devices, Lee probably would have struggled to figure out exactly how to implement the advice given to her—and maybe never finished the manuscript. Fortunately, Hohoff volunteered to take on the editorial responsibility for Lee's book. Hohoff agreed with the concerns about the book's structure but saw great promise in the writing. *That* she could work with. When an editor gets a manuscript that clearly shows care about the craft and an author who is willing to be guided and helped, that's the day the editor remembers why she took on this calling.

Most people don't know who edited a book; only the author's name goes on the cover. In 2015, few knew the name of Tay Hohoff until the publishing money machine kicked in and published, with only a light copyedit, Lee's original manuscript, touting it as "just discovered." Suddenly, the genius of *To Kill a Mockingbird* stood in stark contrast to *Go Set a Watchman,* and the only difference between the two? A little grey-haired woman with a red pen and the ability to see exactly what the book needed.

After that June meeting, Hohoff encouraged Lee and, by the end of the summer, Lee sent a revised manuscript. However, it still lacked unity and had dangling plot lines. Yet Hohoff recognized the spark that only needed to be ignited. Lee had shown that she would put in the time with her writing and willingly accept criticism and advice. Doubtless with this information from Hohoff, Lippincott offered Lee a contract on her book in October of 1957. From that moment for the next three years, until the book was published on July 11, 1960, Hohoff and Lee worked to create what became a masterpiece.

Hohoff recognized in the young woman from Monroeville, Alabama, a suitable voice for a novel set in the South about small town life and people. But her novel needed a big story, an overarching theme, something to keep the story moving. And it needed a unique point of view.

Through hours of discussion, Lee and Hohoff worked out the various problems every writer encounters. At some point, they determined that the real story, the most authentic voice, lay not with the twenty-six-year-old Jean Louise Finch but with the six-year-old tomboy Scout. Although both voices appear in *To Kill a Mockingbird*, the young Scout is the main narrator. Lee worked with the voices, rewriting the novel three times—third-person POV, first-person POV, and finally with a blend. At one point, the story goes that Lee became so frustrated with the writing process that she gathered all the pages and threw the entire draft out her apartment window and into the New York City snow. She called her editor in tears. Hohoff told her in no uncertain terms to go outside, pick up the pages, and keep writing.

How did the editing process morph the story from the racist Atticus that appears in *Watchman* to the Atticus we know and love today—handsome and flawless Gregory Peck in his rocking chair reading to Scout? The study of these two books side by side provides fascinating insights into the editorial process—when an editor asks good questions and when a writer goes back and does the hard work until the manuscript sings.

Several issues may have been at stake at the time Lee was writing. Perhaps with the mood of the country as it was in the early 1960s, Hohoff, savvy editor and longtime publisher, may have seen a need for a kinder and gentler book. Maybe creating Atticus as he appears in *Mockingbird* made for a story that could resonate with the 1960s readers. There were plenty of bigots around; a story about another one with some rants by the man's daughter (as in *Watchman*) perhaps wasn't needed. Maybe Hohoff focused on one thread of the story that made for a stronger book. Maybe Hohoff sensed that when Lee wrote in Scout's voice, something magical happened. I don't know. But comparing the first few chapters of each book reveals that *Watchman* is confusing, and that whatever happened as Lee revised and revised *Mockingbird* brought out brilliant writing.

For example, *Watchman*'s first few pages introduce us to several characters—most of whom are minor. While these folks make an appearance in *Mockingbird,* they aren't important enough to be in the first pages of either book. In *Watchman,* we meet an adult Jean Louise Finch in the second paragraph and hear of her fear of flying, which explains why she's on a train traveling through Alabama. Then there are several paragraphs with the random story of Cousin Joshua who shot at the university president (a story hinted at in *Mockingbird*). In *Watchman,* chapter 2 gives us the story of Atticus; and in chapter 3, we meet Alexandra Finch Hancock (the aunt).

The first chapter of *Watchman* includes several paragraphs that I would call "information dumps": besides the aforementioned random and unimportant information about Cousin Joshua, I learn how a boyfriend named Hank found out about Atticus's arthritis, everything about Hank (including why he has false teeth), and then there's a random conversation in the car ride from the train station that doesn't advance the story or make me particularly like Jean or Hank. And the issue of "show versus tell" rears its ugly head almost immediately. Consider these lines from *Watchman:*

> The countryside and the train had subsided to a gentle roll, and she could see nothing but pastureland and black cows from window to horizon. She wondered why she had never thought her country beautiful.[4]

> *[Thinking about Atticus's arthritis]* She wondered how she would behave when her time came to hurt day in and day out. Hardly like Atticus: if you asked him how he was feeling he would tell you, but he never complained; his disposition remained the same, so in order to find out how he was feeling, you had to ask him.[5]

[And later] Integrity, humor, and patience were the three words for Atticus Finch. ... His private character was his public character.[6]

Note that the last line appears in *Mockingbird*, but comes in a scene where Scout is chatting with Miss Maudie, who says: "Gracious child, I was raveling a thread, wasn't even thinking about your father, but now that I am I'll say this: Atticus Finch is the same in his house as he is on the public streets."[7] The beauty of *To Kill a Mockingbird* is in the beauty of the writing—and that's not something an editor can do. That's the hard work of the writer. The editor can point out the flaws; the author addresses them.

Throughout *To Kill a Mockingbird*, we are shown, not told. There is no single paragraph to tell us how much Scout loves the town or how Atticus rarely shows his feelings. We learn it as we watch the story unfold through charming anecdotes and descriptions of a few years of Scout's young life. In describing Maycomb, Lee treats us with this description in *To Kill a Mockingbird*:

Maycomb was an old town, but it was a tired old town when I first knew it. In rainy weather the streets turned to red slop; grass grew on the sidewalks, the courthouse sagged in the square. Somehow, it was hotter then: a black dog suffered on a summer's day; bony mules hitched to Hoover carts flicked flies in the swelter shade of the live oaks on the square.[8]

Listen to that alliteration: tired town, sagged in the square; suffered on a summer's day; hitched to Hoover carts; flicked flies; swelter shade of the live oaks on the square.

And, of course, there's that voice. The writing is a now-narrator writing as a then-narrator, so the anecdotes and stories are through the eyes of a six-year-old while the verbiage shows a narrator remembering (at times, the adult slips through, as when she says "when I first knew it" describing Maycomb in the example above). The switch from third person (Jean Louise Finch is "she" in *Watchman*) to first person (Scout is "I" in *Mockingbird*) also helps us see the story more clearly through Scout's young eyes. Indeed, there's something about viewing and hearing the complex issues of racism through a child's eyes that resonated even more strongly with the public than Jean Louise Finch's adult diatribes against racism in *Watchman*.

Perhaps that's what Hohoff and Lee talked about over three years' worth of revisions to the manuscript. How much did Hohoff help shape the book from what we have in the one to what we have in the other? Quite a bit, actually. Lee, who was eighty-eight years old at the time of the release of *Go Set a Watchman*, said in a statement, "'In the mid-1950s, I completed a novel called *Go Set a Watchman*. ... It features the character known as Scout as an adult woman, and I thought it a pretty decent effort. My editor, who was taken by the flashbacks to Scout's childhood, persuaded me to write a novel (what became *To Kill a Mockingbird*) from the point of view of the young Scout. I was a first-time writer, so I did as I was told.'"[9]

Hohoff's instincts were correct. Surely there was discussion of the voice and what Hohoff read in those many drafts. The editorial hand indeed had a certain heaviness. But the beauty of the alliterative sentences? The town of Maycomb seen through a six-year-old tomboy's eyes? The fear of Boo Radley and the love for Calpurnia and the adoration of Atticus and the sibling life with Jem? It took Lee many revisions and much frustration and many tears (and a few trips into the snow), but those are all hers.

An editor can't write that. An editor can't revise into that. An editor can only spot where the writer could take the story and then point the way.

When a writer catches the vision and can discuss with others the best way to write the book—from POV to narrator to structure—and then self-edits by doing the detailed work of creating masterful sentences and choosing perfect words and showing instead of telling ... well, that writer is on the way to creating a work he or she can be proud of. And maybe even a masterpiece.

Maxwell Perkins

Maxwell Perkins (1884–1947) was an editor at Charles Scribner's and Sons, but he didn't start off that way. He didn't even study literature or writing in college (Harvard); instead, he studied economics. But his real love was words. After graduation, Perkins went to work for *The New York Times* as the writer who hung around all night and picked up the late-night stories.

Has the editing process changed over the years?

While publishing has changed over the years, the editorial process still pretty much remains the same. The biggest differences are the time available to work on manuscripts, the competition, and the rise of computer.

In the days of Tay Hohoff and Maxwell Perkins, editors were often heavily involved with their authors. Note that Hohoff and Perkins spent *years* on a single manuscript. Everything was done on paper, of course. Revisions were typed and retyped and retyped. Manuscripts went back and forth in boxes by mail. The sheer number of books was far fewer than today, giving the editors and authors more luxury. (The picture of the editor at a martini-and-cigar lunch with an author is not far-fetched.)

Nowadays, publishers are far more lean. Editors are under great pressure and tight deadlines—handling more manuscripts and often more roles than just doing a leisurely content edit. Even though computers and email have sped up communication, the publishers' timelines are tight and fast. It still takes at least a year for a book to get to print, but the actual editorial time has been condensed.

This is why you as a writer being thorough with your self-editing is so important. It sets you above the rest. When a manuscript arrives clean, the editor can more easily keep deadlines and deliver a quality product.

But all that said, editors still do the exact same kind of work. They ask the exact same questions. They look for the exact same grammar and punctuation issues. They keep up with changes in the industry and in the tastes of readers, and they follow vicissitudes of grammar as language changes.

Books change, readers' tastes change, but the basics of what makes a well-written book always stay the same.

He eventually got a job at Scribner's in the advertising department where he spent four and a half years before ascending to the hallowed fifth floor—the editorial floor. When he finally got there, he wasn't an editor. Instead, he cut his teeth as a proofreader. For the most part, his duties were limited to proofreading galleys—long printed sheets, each containing the equivalent of three book pages—and to other random chores.

A regular Scribner author named Shane Leslie became friends with a young author from Minnesota. Leslie sent this young author's manuscript to the editors at Scribner. It got passed around (no one liked it) until it ended up on Perkins's desk. While he liked it, he was forced to write to the author and decline it (the lowly proofreader didn't have much sway at first). But Perkins saw something in the writing, and the rejection letter held out hope and encouragement to the young man who went to work revising.

The manuscript came back much improved, and Perkins went to work doing everything he could (and it was a *lot*) to get Scribner's to publish it. At one tense editorial meeting, he said, "My feeling is that a publisher's first allegiance is to talent. And if we aren't going to publish talent like this, it is a very serious thing."[10]

The young author was F. Scott Fitzgerald. The book was *This Side of Paradise* (Scribner's 1920).

At this point, I need to stop for a moment and just bask in the wonder of this event. What if Perkins had not encouraged Fitzgerald? What if he had not made such a strong argument for the book? Perkins saw great writing, he saw talent, and he did all that he could to make the book happen. Thus, we can thank Maxwell Perkins for believing in Fitzgerald and helping get his debut novel published.

After the great commercial success of *This Side of Paradise*, the publisher was ready for more. Fitzgerald wrote short stories and another book for Scribner's. Eventually, he told Perkins about his next project, a book for which he had several possible titles, including *Among the Ash-Heaps and Millionaires, Trimalchio in West Egg, Trimalchio, On the Road to West Egg, Gold-hatted Gatsby,* and *The High-bouncing Lover.* (In case you're wondering [I did], Trimalchio was a character in a Latin work by Petronius from the first century A.D.—a man given to hosting lavish parties. Hence, the reason for that terrible title, although without explanation, it was lost on me.) As you can imagine, there was much discussion about the title in the editorial offices and with Fitzgerald himself. Anyway, you and I know this book as *The Great Gatsby.*

When the manuscript finally landed on Perkins's desk, Fitzgerald sent a letter explaining that he wasn't happy with the middle of the book. "Do tell me the absolute truth, *your first impression of the book,* & tell me anything that bothers you in it."[11] Perkins reported that he loved it, but was concerned about the titular character. Perkins felt that he could spot Tom Buchanan if he met him on the street, but Gatsby's character was vague: "The reader's eyes can never quite focus upon him, his outlines are dim."[12] Perkins suggested that Fitzgerald describe Gatsby as distinctly as he had described Tom and Daisy.

Perkins also understood that Gatsby's past needed to maintain a certain air of mystery, but he didn't want to shortchange the readers. He saw the complete lack of explanation of Gatsby as a cause for confusion in the story. Perkins was also concerned that the parts of Gatsby's past that Fitzgerald did divulge were all dumped together in one spot. Perkins suggested that Fitzgerald also pepper that information throughout the book.

Fitzgerald began his revisions—from the title page. He chose the title Perkins liked, *The Great Gatsby.* He responded to everything Max suggested. He broke up the block of information about Gatsby's past and sprinkled the details into other chapters. He made Gatsby's claim of his time at Oxford come up in several conversations. And one key change was stimulated by something Perkins had said. Fitzgerald gave a certain "tick" to Gatsby. In the original manuscript, Gatsby had called people "old man" or "old fellow." Perkins liked it when Gatsby called people "old sport," so Fitzgerald tossed it everywhere into Gatsby's conversations. The phrase thus became such a strong part of Gatsby's manner that in the Plaza Hotel scene, it provoked Tom Buchanan:

"That's a great expression of yours, isn't it?" said Tom sharply.

"What is?" [said Gatsby]

"All this 'old sport' business. Where'd you pick that up?"[13]

Through the process of rewriting and revising, Perkins encouraged, advised, and offered suggestions but always knew that the brilliance lay with Fitzgerald. He simply wanted to make what was already great that much better. Perkins knew genius when he saw it and couched any criticisms in much-needed approval. (If you've been edited, you know that it's tough to see the negative comments, the places where something doesn't work, the red-penned suggestions. To first hear your editor's overall positive opinion helps you deal with the negatives.)

In my editing class, I teach my students about the value of positive comments. Many are writers themselves, which means they have a foundation on what good writing looks like. In the first section of the class, I teach them content editing of fiction and nonfiction. In both cases, they receive real manuscripts from real people on which they will act as content editors.

I teach them, as editors of these pages entrusted to them, to give the "Perkins touch." As my students make the electronic side comments on the pages, I require them to make a minimum of three positive comments out of the total of at least twelve suggestions or critiques. Then, when they write their overview letter back to their author, they must begin by giving the author positive feedback. I challenge my students to put themselves in the shoes of the person who will receive their letters.

But then, of course, Perkins would not be an editor if he did not help his authors see places that still needed work—and *every* book needs something, even the ones from the greatest writers. In his editorial letter back to Fitzgerald, he gave positive comments then dug into the detail. The book is the author's book, yes, but the editor has a huge amount of influence. Why? Because the editor is the author's best reader. Perkins cared as much about Tom and Daisy and Gatsby and Nick and Jordan and Myrtle as Fitzgerald did. Your editor will be as intimately involved with the text as you are—and this should be a great relief to you.

Perkins and Fitzgerald worked hard, writing back and forth, making revisions. Of course, it's easy to say how valuable that process was when we know that the book has become a classic. But upon publication, *The Great Gatsby* wasn't well received. In April 1925, a review of the book in the *St. Louis Dispatch* said, "Altogether it seems to us this book is a minor performance. At the moment, its author seems a bit bored and tired and cynical. There is no ebullience here, nor is there any mellowness or profundity. For our part, *The Great Gatsby* might just as well be called *Ten Nights on Long Island*."[14]

Ouch.

By the time Fitzgerald died in 1940, he had made a little over thirteen dollars in royalties on the book.

But the book stood the test of time. Falling into line behind various books that describe a time gone by (*Moby-Dick,* for example), *The Great Gatsby* became iconic because it deftly offers us a glimpse into a world not our own and yet very much our own. The book's theme speaks to what it was like to be young in America during the Jazz Age, while still considering transcendent human issues of privilege and loneliness and the ultimate emptiness of great wealth.

Since 1925, Scribner's has sold more than 25 million copies of the book, selling about five hundred thousand a year in recent years. But Fitzgerald didn't live to see his book become a best-seller as he died in 1940. Neither did Perkins, who died in 1947. I'm sure both died thinking that the book was of no value, smarting from the poor reviews.

However, their hard work was well worth it. For that, we as readers can be grateful. Fitzgerald (and Perkins) gave us a masterpiece of Americana.

I share these stories to show you how great works don't spring from their authors ready-made and error-free. They need work. They require other readers to point out places that need clarity, to help guide the focus and theme, to determine the best voice. Listen carefully to the advice you hear. Take the time to try other perspectives or voices in your work. See if a change unlocks your writing and makes it come alive.

Above all, continue to work hard on that piece you're writing. You don't know if your book will, like *To Kill a Mockingbird,* become an instant best-seller and change the course of history; or if it will, like *The Great Gatsby,* become a classic, seen for its brilliance long after you're gone. Or maybe the only people who will read it and be changed by it are the folks in your critique group. Keep your perspective. Do the hard work because it matters; the words matter; you and your story matter.

You've completed your big-picture self-editing. That means that if your manuscript is fiction, the book should have the plot and pacing on target, enticing characters and dialog, and a strong beginning and ending; if it's nonfiction, the organization is clear and logical, the readers are gaining what you want them to, and the beginning and ending are solid. Now, when you feel like your book is in its close-to-final shape, we can move on to the next phase. We're ready to format your manuscript.

4
Copyediting:
Formatting Your Manuscript

Y ou have cut and pasted and moved and revised the big-picture elements of your manuscript. The next step is to format it to industry standards. I advise formatting before you start reading to copyedit.

Longtime author and editor Andy Scheer one day posted on Facebook how thrilled he was to receive a manuscript to edit that had been formatted correctly. I dropped him a note to ask, from his perspective, what constituted a manuscript that is "formatted correctly." Here's the list he sent me.

- Manuscript is .doc or .docx
- 12-pt Times New Roman
- Double-spaced copy
- No extra space between paragraphs
- 1-inch margins
- No double spaces between sentences
- Paragraphs indented—but NOT with tabs or spacing
- Page headers with page numbers
- Page break between chapters
- Front matter completed (title page, copyright page, table of contents if needed)
- Copyright page includes copyright info for all Bible versions quoted, especially the default Bible translation[15]

Let's walk through each of these bullet points individually. I'll help out with the basics. Any technical notes are on my website (lindaktaylor.com/word-by-word); go there for the individual steps. Several items on the list can be handled with creating a standardized template. Let's do that first.

If you need technical help ...

Microsoft Word can be quite a mystery if you're not used to digging around inside it. Thus, to help you with formatting and other issues that I suggest in this chapter, I have created some step-by-step guidelines for you.

However, because Microsoft Word periodically updates and often moves buttons around or makes other changes, I cannot include everything and if I did, this book would soon be woefully out of date. Because I don't want that to happen, I'm including the technical information at a page on my blog (lindaktaylor.com/word-by-word).

Throughout this book, you will see notes in bold in various places suggesting that you go to the website to locate the steps to do what I suggest. Go there if you need any kind of help and, if you're still stuck, use the contact form on the website to write me. I'll be happy to try to help.

Build Your Template

Creating a template handles several of the bulleted items on the list right away. You can deal with these basic formatting issues with using a couple of dialog boxes. Follow the instructions for **Technical Tip: Creating Your Manuscript Template** on the website where I walk you through the steps in Microsoft Word.

Trust me, having a template that's your own, that has all of the settings you need already embedded, will be a huge help to you. After you've set up the template, do a "Save As" and call it "My awesome template" or something like that. Every time you start a new book or a new story, open this template, do another "Save As" to save that piece of writing with whatever title you want to give it. That way you'll always preserve the settings you created in your template and won't have to redo all those settings every time for every piece of writing.

If you don't have Microsoft Word on your computer

Understandably, you may not have Microsoft Word on your computer (usually it is in Microsoft Office). Because Word is the industry standard, and because you will eventually send your manuscript electronically, your manuscript will need to be in .doc or .docx format. However, you don't need to purchase Word if you don't have it. Many computer at libraries have the program, or you may know someone who has it on a computer.

Build your template on that other computer, and plan to work with your manuscript there as you finish. Each time, save your document in your email, on a thumb drive, or on Google docs. Use that computer to make the final touches on your manuscript. It may be awkward, but it will be well worth it for the sake of getting your manuscript into the right hands.

The .doc or .docx extension should automatically appear with any document you create in Microsoft Word. Look at the name of your template; it should say "whatevertitleyougaveit.doc" or ".docx."

Once you have that template ready, along the Home ribbon at the top of your screen, Microsoft Word has gives you buttons for some basic styles that will probably be the ones you will use most. Most everything that you type will be in the "Normal" style. You could go ahead and type right into your new template all those words just waiting to be put to paper! Always do a "Save As" with a new title to preserve your clear template.

For now, keep that clear template open in one window, and open your WIP in another. Transfer your WIP onto the new template. Type Control + A to highlight the entire manuscript, then Control + C (or right click your mouse and choose "Copy"). (On a Mac, press Command + A to highlight everything, and then copy with Command + C.) Go over to that blank new template, put your cursor at the starting point, type Control + V (or right click and choose "Paste"). Be sure to choose the option that says "Merge Formatting." That way your old formatting from your previous document will try to follow the new guidelines in your template (for example, the "Normal" text that you may have typed, say, single spaced in your original document will come over as "Normal" text but will automatically become double spaced because that's how you set up "Normal" in the template).

A few items to check: If you were in the habit of indenting your paragraphs with a tab, when you paste your manuscript into your template (that is set for automatic indents on paragraphs), you may end up with double indents. The best way to fix that is to navigate to the Home ribbon. In the Paragraph section you'll see a button top right that looks like a backward P. Click that and you'll see all of the embedded material in the document (your spaces will appear like dots, your tabs will appear like arrows pointing to the right). When you see these random indents, remove them. If you have zillions of them, do a quick fix. Check the website for **Technical Tip: Removing Tabbed Indents**.

No Double Spaces Between Sentences

If you're typing two spaces between sentences, it's probably because you learned to type on a typewriter. Typewriters only had one font, one size. Each letter, punctuation mark, and space took up the same amount of space. You learned to put in two spaces in order to make it clear where sentences ended. Computers have proportional typefaces, so that second space between sentences is no longer needed.

If you're still hitting that space bar twice, don't worry about the frustration of trying to retrain yourself. Just type your piece, double spaces and all. We'll do a quick fix afterward. See on the website, **Technical Tip: Fixing Double Spacing between Sentences.** Follow those instructions and *voilà!* Easy.

Page Headers with Page Numbers

Picture this: An agent has an office with piles of manuscripts—some on the desk, some on the floor, some on the file cabinet, some on the windowsill. While he or she may be extremely organized, anything can happen—the cat might run through and mess up the piles, or a sudden gust through an open window whips the piles of paper into a snowstorm across the office floor. You don't want your unnumbered and unlabeled pages to become an impossible puzzle to put back together, especially when it's easy to put your last name, your book title, and your page number on every page. You do it once, and it will appear on every page. See the website for **Technical Tip: Page Headers and Page Numbers** to help you out.

Note: Be sure that you follow the guidelines if you are submitting the manuscript to a certain agent or acquisitions editor. They usually have submission guidelines on their websites. Some may ask you to include your name and/or the title of the manuscript along with the page number. Others may ask for other information to be on each page. If you're not sure, at least include your last name and page numbers in the headers on your manuscript.

Page Break Between Chapters

It's important that each new chapter start on its own page, but don't keep doing a return after the last line on a page until a new page appears. Instead, after that line, when you're ready to start a new chapter, insert a page break. Check out the website for **Technical Tip: Page Break between Chapters.**

But here's a *major and important tip* that will help you in some of the other steps. Say you've done a page break and you're starting a new chapter. Wherever you have a chapter title, double click on the entire title so that Word is highlighting it. Then on that Home ribbon where you see the Styles, click on the style labeled "Heading 1." Do this procedure for every chapter title. That will format each chapter title with a special style tag (by default, it will probably center it and make it a larger font, all fine). This formatting will help you when you go to create the table of contents.

Front Matter Completed

Whether you're turning in your book to an editor or preparing to self-publish it, make sure that all of the front and back matter (referring to material that comes before and after the text itself) is included *and* in the correct order.

Here's the order (if you have extra pieces, refer to the *Chicago Manual of Style* for a complete list). You probably won't have all of these items. The only two you *must* have are the title page and copyright page. A nonfiction book will generally need a table of contents; you may or may not have one in a fiction book. Also, remember to put a page break between each section.

Front matter

- ✔ Title page (*must have*)

- ✔ Copyright page (*must have*)

- ✔ Dedication

- ✔ Table of Contents (*standard in nonfiction; optional if fiction*)

- ✔ Foreword

- ✔ Preface

- ✔ Acknowledgments (*if not part of the Preface or in the back matter*)

- ✔ Introduction (*if not part of the text*)

Back matter

- ✔ Acknowledgments (*if not in front matter—or you might include an About the Author page here*)

✔ Appendixes in order

✔ Notes

✔ Glossary

✔ Bibliography or References

✔ Indexes

Title page

It's best not to use any of the "Cover Page" options that Word gives you; it's better to be simple. Visually center the material vertically, and use the centering button to center your lines horizontally. On the title page, include your title, subtitle, and name (as you want it to appear on the cover). Do not type the copyright symbol on the cover page; it is not necessary to "protect yourself," and you'll look amateurish if you include it.

Copyright page

After you've finished the title page, insert a page break and begin your copyright page. On the first line, type "parenthesis C parenthesis," and you probably will automatically get the © symbol. If you don't, navigate to the "Insert" tab, and on the far right of that ribbon is the "Symbol" button. Click on the down arrow and a few recent symbols may show up. If you don't see that symbol, click on "More symbols" and amongst all the offerings is the copyright symbol. After that symbol, put the current year and your name, like this:

Copyright © 2017 Linda K. Taylor

It's helpful if you include the copyright lines of any material for which you needed to get permission to quote. And while you don't need to request permission to quote verses from Bibles, you still need to include the copyright lines of Bible versions you quote. Remember that Andy Scheer pointed out that a well-formatted manuscript has a copyright page that "includes copyright info for all Bible versions quoted, especially the default Bible translation (advice applies to all quoted material)."

As you wrote your document, you kept track of your source(s) for Bible verses—that is, what Bible version you were quoting from (you did, didn't you?). Perhaps you just typed the verses from your well-worn Bible. Or maybe you copied and pasted from a particular version from BibleGateway.com or some other digital Bible source. Or maybe you quoted from several different Bible versions because you liked the nuances of the way various versions translate your key verses.

If you know that you quoted from just one Bible version, then on the copyright page, create a line that says:

All Scripture quotations taken from...

Go to that Bible you were quoting from and open to its copyright page. In my New Living Translation, it says this:

When the *Holy Bible,* New Living Translation, is quoted, one of the following credit lines must appear on the copyright page or title page of the work.

Then follow three options. The first would be used if all of the verses you quoted were from the New Living Translation—and in this case, throughout your manuscript, you don't need to put NLT after all of the references since your default version is NLT. Thus, (Gen. 1:1) or (Genesis 1:1) is all you need; no need to include a Bible version. In this case, the NLT says to write the following on your copyright page:

Scripture quotations are taken from the *Holy Bible,* New Living Translation, copyright © 1996, 2004, 2007, 2013 by Tyndale House Foundation. Used by permission of Tyndale House Publishers, Inc., Carol Stream, Illinois 60188. All rights reserved.

If the NLT is your default and the only version you used, you would type the above exact line onto your copyright page. And, incidentally, they are giving you permission without you having to ask for it. They list caveats to their permissions policy on their copyright page, which state that you can do this without officially asking for permission "up to and inclusive of five hundred (500) verses without express written permission of the publisher, provided that the verses quoted do not account for more than 25 percent of the work in which they are quoted, and provided that a complete book of the Bible is not quoted."

Let's consider another scenario. Perhaps the New Living Translation was the main one you used, but you sprinkled in a couple other versions (maybe you wanted to quote one verse from the King James Version). In that case, you don't need to put NLT after all of the references, but you do need to make sure the King James Version is noted at that reference. "The LORD is my shepherd; I shall not want" (Psalm 23:1 KJV). On your copyright page, you will choose this line from that NLT copyright page:

> Unless otherwise indicated, all Scripture quotations are taken from…(etc.)

And then you'll also include a copyright line from the KJV Bible.

> Scripture quotations marked KJV are taken from the King James Version…(etc., with the copyright line from your Bible)

If you used a variety of versions, make sure that after every verse, you note the reference and the version. After each of the quoted verses, you would have, for example, (Genesis 1:1 NIV) and in another place perhaps (Romans 5:8 NLT) and in yet another (Philippians 1:5 KJV). Now, on the copyright page, include the copyright lines for each Bible. These will be easy to locate if you were typing from your Bibles—the information is on the copyright page. In the above scenario, you'll have three lines on your copyright page, one for the NLT, one for the NIV, and one for the KJV. In this case, then, you'll use the next option from that NLT copyright page that says:

Scripture quotations marked NLT are taken from the
Holy Bible, New Living Translation...(etc.)

(Then follow with the appropriate copyright lines from all the other versions.)

If you're using an electronic source with various Bible versions to copy and paste your verses (such as Bible Gateway, You Version, Olive Tree, Logos, Bible Soft), draw the Bible version's copyright line from there. On Bible Gateway, for example, call up a verse, choose your version, and scroll to the bottom of the window just below the quoted verse. The program provides the Bible version copyright information. Copy and paste it from there. In addition, each Bible has a website (usually connected to the publisher of that Bible) and on that website are the exact lines that are required for the copyright page.

Be careful, however. Some Bible versions are updated. That NIV that you have had for years is most likely the 1983 version; the one on Bible Gateway is the 2011 version. Make sure that you don't quote from your Bible and then try to lift the line from BibleGateway as that would not be correct.

I can't begin to tell you how happy folks at the other end will be that you took care of all of these details. The copy editors will check all of your Bible verse quotations and references to make sure they're correct, but you do a great service when you provide them with the Bible version. Many times I've copyedited manuscripts where I've had to dig around in various electronic sources to try to locate the verse as the author typed it—working my way through every Bible version to try to find a match.

Don't make your copy editor do that.

This advice to be careful and to keep track of sources applies not just to Bible texts but to *anything from which you quote.* If you're quoting from other sources—books, magazines, newspapers, articles, blogs—keep track and make sure to source the material correctly. Sometimes this material needs to go on the copyright page; sometimes it will be in your footnotes, endnotes, or bibliography. Keep that information on hand.

On the copyright page, include some standard information such as this:

When the book is published, the publisher will take care of putting on the copyright page their boiler-plate copyright page information in place, their Library of Congress information, the printing numbers, etc. You just need to provide the basics.

Table of contents

You can prepare a table of contents a couple of ways. One way is to hand type each entry. After the copyright page, insert a page break, start at the top line and type "Contents" or "Table of Contents." Insert a return, and then begin by typing the first entry that appears next in the book (such as an Introduction or a Prologue). An easy way to hand prepare a table of contents is to split the screen. Place your cursor where you want to type "Chapter One" or "Chapter 1." Then, navigate to the "View" tab. On that ribbon, you'll see a button about halfway across that says "Split." If you click that, a bar will appear that splits your screen. Keep the top window intact and viewing the table of contents page while you use the bottom window to scroll through the document. Scroll to the start of chapter 1 and type the title into your table of contents. Start the next line in the table of contents, and drop to the bottom screen and continue to scroll until you get to the next chapter. When you're finished, hit that same button (which now says "Remove Split"), and the split will disappear.

If you want to use Word's table of contents feature, check the website for **Technical Tip: Building a Table of Contents.** Because you still may change your chapter titles, and because it is difficult to edit this automatically entered table of contents, if you want to use this tool, use it at the very end after you've proofread and you're sure the chapters are titled as you want them.

Foreword, preface, introduction, or prologue?

You may or may not include each of these items in your manuscript, but let's make sure that you are using the terminology correctly and that what you write fits the category.

A *foreword* (not a "forward") is written by someone else. This person might be a celebrity or someone well-known in the field about which you're writing. This person tells your audience why your book is valuable and worth their time to read. It amounts to an endorsement.

A *preface* is written by you to acquaint your readers with some interesting information about you, how you came to write the book, or other interesting circumstances surrounding the book's creation. This could also include information such as "How to Use This Book" if that is necessary.

An *introduction* gets into the content of your book. You want readers to read it because it sets them up for what is to come. For instance, if your potential reader is standing in the bookstore and has lifted your book from the shelf, he or she is going to look at the cover, read the back cover copy, and then open to the introduction. You want to explain to the reader exactly what the book is offering. In the Introduction to this book, I described my target audience and said exactly what my readers can expect to get from this book.

A *prologue* is similar to an introduction, except that if you have a prologue at the beginning of your book, you should also include an epilogue at the end.

Style of footnotes/endnotes and bibliography entries

If you will be using footnotes or endnotes, use Word program helps as noted in **Technical Tip: Inserting Footnotes and Endnotes** on my website.

Be sure to follow the style guide for the type of document you're writing. If you're writing a book, use *Chicago Manual of Style*; if you're writing for newspapers or magazines, use AP; if it's an academic piece, use MLA or APA. Get the basic styles for all of these at the Purdue OWL (stands for Online Writing Lab) website or from the publication or publishing house style manual. If you are writing with a particular publisher in mind, ask for a copy of their house style guide. Each has its own way of treating sources, and every type of source has its own way of being handled, *and* you will need to know how to source the material as a note and how to do so in a bibliography or resource list.

Do your best, but don't worry too much about the details. Most copy editors live and breathe this stuff and know just what to do to make these entries perfect. They will happily find and fix any flaws.

Having your manuscript clean and formatted this way makes the next phase of the process easier. Let's move on to reading word by word.

5
Copyediting:
Reading Word by Word

During big-picture editing, you don't pay attention to minor errors—awkward or run-on sentences, dangling modifiers, punctuation or spelling errors. I advised you to mark these if you run across them in your content edit but not to fix them. Save all those fixes for this stage when you will read word by word—when you copyedit.

If you have the time, let your book sit for a while (I know, I made you let it sit before content editing; this self-editing process *does* take a long time). The reason I say to wait is because your eyes and brain know your manuscript too well. You know what it says and so can easily read over simple copyediting mistakes because your mind will fill in what you know you meant to say. Let it rest as long as possible—a couple weeks is ideal. Then you will see the manuscript with fresh eyes.

As I suggested when you were content editing, *print out your manuscript,* especially if you made large changes during your content-editing phase. You can read on screen, but you will see more problems on a printed copy than you do on your screen. Seriously, now is not the time to worry about using paper or ink. You can recycle. If you want your book to be the best it can be, use every tool available—even if it means going through a few reams of paper and some ink cartridges. A reader of my blog named Sara offered this advice:

> Self-editing is not a process to be taken lightly. It is too easy to miss some rather bodacious and comical mistakes. If you do address this, advise your readers to set aside their "final" manuscript IN PRINT and

NOT on the screen, for at least three months before doing the final proofreading.

If they don't, they'll miss a priceless error like this one: ten girl year-old. Never saw it until I got myself a copy to read. Had to go back and revise that entire page! Self-editing is not to be taken lightly.[16]

Sara is right. Don't take this process lightly. As important as content editing is, this copyediting phase is just as important. You may not have the luxury of waiting three months, but do let the manuscript rest as long as possible.

After I completed the content revisions to this book, I waited two weeks before even looking at it again. Only then did I print it out and begin copyediting. I couldn't believe all the red marks I made as I read. I needed transitions. I had many unclear antecedents (what is "this" or "it" referring to?). I needed to delete many instances of my overuse of the word *so* (one of my editing students mentioned that after she read the manuscript). When I used the Microsoft Word tools to search for the word *so*, it told me, "Too many to count. You use that word a lot!" Yikes! I also found unclear sentences that needed minor revisions. I didn't find many spelling errors, though (thankfully). Oh, and lots of passive voice sentences were fixed (I mean, I fixed lots of passive voice sentences).

In the copyediting pass on your manuscript, you move in close and ask questions like:

✔ Is the sentence reading right? Or is it a run-on sentence? Or does it have a dangling or misplaced modifiers? Or is the wording awkward as I read?

✔ Is that the right word, and is it spelled correctly?

✔ Is the dialog punctuated correctly?

✔ Is that date for that historical event correct? Is that person's / company's / organization's name spelled right?

✔ Is there too much passive voice that could be changed to active voice?

✔ Does the manuscript need better transitions?

✔ Is that Bible reference and/or quotation accurate?

✔ Do the entries in my table of contents match the titles at the beginnings of the chapters? (I can't tell you how often this is not the case in manuscripts I've copyedited. The author will make a change in one place but forget to make the same change in the other.)

✔ Are the facts and statistics correct and verifiable?

✔ Does all of the quoted material have source notations? Are quotations of more than five lines set apart in block text? Are sources to be noted as footnotes or endnotes or in text? Does the bibliography / references page list everything in the notes?

✔ Also take note of your "tics"—what you do in your writing that can be problematic. Maybe, like me, overuse of a particular word (mine was *so*). Or too many em-dashes or exclamation points. Once you know what you tend to do, search and destroy.

This chapter gives you a few basic pieces of grammar advice. I focus on the kinds of problems that are common in the manuscripts I've copyedited over the years.

Basic Grammar You Need to Know

You don't need to be a grammarian to copyedit your book, but it will help to know a few basics and get a little practice so you know what to watch for in your manuscript. I've been copyediting for nearly three decades; thus, I'm going to give you a quick overview, along with a few examples, of the types of errors I see most. I don't address every nuance of grammar (we have books for that). Instead, I want to simply cover some basics.

You may run across some questions particular to your manuscript, and that's where *Chicago Manual of Style* or other style guides can help you. For our basic purposes here, use the following points as a checklist and you'll have covered 90 percent of what to fix to create a clean manuscript.

Let's get right to it! (Note to you dear readers: Perhaps you don't want to read this entire section right now. I'm hoping that it's more of a resource for you. Scan the subheads to see what I'm addressing, then go back and focus on what you need when you need it.)

A. Spelling and correct word usage

Watch for confusing words. If you're not 100 percent sure, look it up. A dictionary is your best friend. I always have the correct dictionary close by (use the one determined by your client's style guide; barring that, use dictionary.com and have it open in another window as you work). Look at the following sentences. The underlined word is the correct word. Are those the words you'd have chosen?

The book (affected, effected) her spiritual life, and it had a similar (affect, effect) on Brian.

Is there (any way, anyway) you could give me a list? I need to go to the store (any way, anyway).

Carol was tired; she decided to go (lie, lay) down.

Sean will (lie, lay) the book on the table for you.

My new car can go (farther, further) on a tank of gas (then, than) my old car.

After you calm down, we can talk (farther, further).

B. Commas

Commas are by far the most confusing for writers (and even copy editors)—and everyone seems to have their own way of using commas. I'm giving you some basic comma usage rules for most of the situations you'll run into.

(1) Use a comma to set off introductory phrases and clauses.

Wrong: At least once a year my family goes camping.
Right: At least once a year, my family goes camping.

Wrong: Until refrigeration was invented people used iceboxes.
Right: Until refrigeration was invented, people used iceboxes.

Wrong: After all everyone will hear about it sooner or later.
Right: After all, everyone will hear about it sooner or later.

(2) Use a comma before a coordinating conjunction (for, and, nor, but, or, so, yet) that links two complete sentences.

Wrong: I like to go shopping yet I hate going alone.
Right: I like to go shopping, yet I hate going alone.

Wrong: I want to take a vacation this year but I should save my money for a new car.
Right: I want to take a vacation this year, but I should save my money for a new car.

(3) Don't use a comma before a linking conjunction (if, though, whenever, because, since, while, before, when).

Wrong: I will walk to work, because the repair shop is just around the corner.
Right: I will walk to work because the repair shop is just around the corner.

Wrong: I always get frustrated, whenever I have to learn a new computer program.
Right: I always get frustrated whenever I have to learn a new computer program.

Wrong: I will try the new program, if you will train me.
Right: I will try the new program if you will train me.

(4) Use a comma to separate items in a series ("serial" or Oxford vs. not).

These types of commas refer to whether or not you put a comma before the word *and* in a series. Style guides and publishers determine this for works they publish. As you're copyediting, choose one and be consistent. The standard in *Chicago Manual of Style* is to use the serial comma; the standard in AP style (writing for newspapers or magazines) is not to use the serial comma.

Serial comma: For lunch today we had sandwiches, melon, cut vegetables, and cookies.
No serial comma: For lunch today we had sandwiches, melon, cut vegetables and cookies.

(5) If a name is the only thing in the world described by an identifier, use commas before and after the name. If not, don't use commas.

Wrong: I went to see the movie, *Rogue One*, with my friend, Ari.

This is wrong, unless *Rogue One* is the only movie in the world and Ari is the writer's only friend. This should be:

Right: I went to see the movie *Rogue One* with my friend Ari.

But look at this:
Right: I went to see the latest Star Wars movie, *Rogue One*, with my oldest friend, Ari.

You need commas around the movie name because this and only this (at least at this point in time) is the *latest* movie in the Star Wars franchise, and a comma before "Ari" because she and only she can be the writer's *oldest* friend.

Right: My daughter, Courtney, is awesome. (If writer has just one daughter.)

Right: My daughter Courtney is awesome. (If writer has more than one daughter.)

(6) Think essential vs. nonessential when considering whether to put commas around phrases.

If the phrase can be set apart in parentheses, it's nonessential and therefore should be set apart with commas. It's nonessential if it isn't vital information for the sentence, and if the sentence would make sense without it.

Wrong: Dr. Hensley author of *Finding Success with Your Dream Writing Projects* is excited about his latest book coming out next summer.

Right: Dr. Hensley, author of *Finding Success with Your Dream Writing Projects,* is excited about his latest book coming out next summer.

The phrase "author of *Finding Success with Your Dream Writing Projects*" is nonessential because, to remove it doesn't change the meaning of the sentence. You might still say, "Dr. Hensley is excited about his latest book coming out next summer." That sentence makes sense without the nonessential phrase. Thus, you put commas around that phrase.

Wrong: Dave's favorite food which he cooks every Saturday night is deep-dish pizza.

Right: Dave's favorite food, which he cooks every Saturday night, is deep-dish pizza.

The phrase "which he cooks every Saturday night" is nonessential because, to remove it, doesn't change the meaning. You might still say, "Dave's favorite food is deep-dish pizza." That sentence makes sense without the nonessential phrase. Thus, you put commas around it.

Wrong: The place, where Dave likes to eat his pizza, is in the comfortable chair by the big-screen television.

Right: The place where Dave likes to eat his pizza is in the comfortable chair by the big-screen television.

At first glance, you might think that you should put commas around "where Dave likes to eat his pizza." However, to do that would mean that phrase is nonessential; without it, you have the sentence, "The place is in the comfortable chair by the big-screen television," which doesn't make sense. Thus, the phrase "where Dave likes to eat his pizza" is essential to this sentence and should *not* have commas around it.

(7) Watch out for comma splices.

Comma splices occur when you link two independent clauses with a comma.

Wrong: He used to be a biology major, now he's studying professional writing.

The above sentence is wrong because both clauses can stand alone as full sentences. Such stand-alone clauses should not be joined by a comma. Fix this problem several ways:

Right: He used to be a biology major. Now he's studying professional writing. (Use a period to separate the two independent clauses and revise the capitalization.)

Right: He used to be a biology major; now he's studying professional writing. (Use a semi-colon to separate the two independent clauses.)

Right: He used to be a biology major, but now he's studying professional writing. (Use a comma, but add a coordinating conjunction.)

Right: He used to be a biology major—now he's studying professional writing. (Use an em-dash to separate the independent clauses.)

How do you choose? Read the sentences aloud in context and choose the version that best suits the context, the style of writing, and your ear.

(8) Be careful using commas along with quotations.

Wrong: "The way the Cubs have been playing, they might just go to the World Series," the coach said, "Wouldn't that be something for the record books!"
Right: "The way the Cubs have been playing, they might just go to the World Series," the coach said. "Wouldn't that be something for the record books!"

The comma after "said" must be a period because clearly the coach's two statements are separate. It helps to read dialog aloud as you copyedit. Your ear will help tell you how the punctuation should be.

Right: "The way the Cubs have been playing, they might just go to the World Series," the coach said, "which would be something for the record books!"

In this example, the comma after "said" is correct because the "said" break appears in the middle of the coach's statement.

(9) Also watch for the word "however." It's different from "but" and "yet."

Use a comma after the word "however." If the word appears in the middle of a sentence, see the following examples.

Wrong: The weather is great today, however it's supposed to rain tomorrow.

To correct this sentence, do one of the following:

Right: The weather is great today, but it's supposed to rain tomorrow.

Right: The weather is great today; however, it's supposed to rain tomorrow.

Right: The weather is great today. However, it's supposed to rain tomorrow.

(10) Use a comma to set off phrases that contrast the main part of the sentence.

Wrong: The test is next week not this week.
Right: The test is next week, not this week.

Wrong: The pizza is fresh not frozen.
Right: The pizza is fresh, not frozen.

(11) Put a comma before the word *too*.

Wrong: The CEO was fired; his assistant was too. The CFO left town. The bookkeeper did too.

Right: The CEO was fired; his assistant was, too. The CFO left town. The bookkeeper did, too.

(12) Be careful when using commas with adjectives.

Do not place commas between adjectives when one or more of them refers to number, color, age, material, or ethnicity:

Wrong: three, yellow roses
Right: three yellow roses (*number and color*)

Wrong: old, silk blouse
Right: old silk blouse (*age and material*)

Wrong: tall, Hispanic female
Right: tall Hispanic female (*ethnicity*)

Wrong: bright, blue sky
Right: bright blue sky (*color*)

Coordinate adjectives are adjectives of equal importance. You can tell equality if you can reverse the order of the adjectives and put *and* between them. If so, you need the comma.

Wrong: A ghostly form appeared at the end of the long narrow hallway.
Right: A ghostly form appeared at the end of the long, narrow hallway.

Put a comma between "long" and "narrow" because you can reverse the order of the adjectives, add "and," and it makes sense. In other words, you could say "the narrow and long hallway." Both of these adjectives are of equal importance. Put a comma between those adjectives.

Wrong: I wear my yellow, silk sweater to lift my spirits.
Right: I wear my yellow silk sweater to lift my spirits.

If you can't reverse the order and use *and*, then you don't need a comma. In this example (besides the fact that we have the rule about not using commas with colors), you wouldn't say "yellow and silk sweater," so don't use a comma.

C. Semi-colons and colons

(1) Place semi-colons between two independent clauses when they aren't separated by a conjunction such as *and* or *but.*

I preferred the presentation by Tamara's dad; he's a scientist.

Each clause in this sentence, "I preferred the presentation by Tamara's dad," and "he's a scientist" could each stand alone. To use a comma would create a comma splice, so use a semi-colon (or a period, or an em-dash). Semi-colons separate independent clauses when you don't want a full stop, which a period would signal.

I went to the book reading expecting to be intrigued; I wasn't disappointed.

Each clause in this sentence, "I went to the book reading expecting to be intrigued," and "I wasn't disappointed" could stand alone. This is an example where a period might create an unnecessary stop; the semi-colon shows the close relationship of these two sentences.

(2) Use semi-colons to separate items in a series when there are phrases with commas or other punctuation in them.

The American flag is red, white, and blue; the Japanese flag is white and red; and the German flag is red, gold, and black.

With the plethora of commas in this sentences separating the colors, it makes sense to use semi-colons to separate the clauses focusing on three types of flags.

All I remembered was that one student, whose name I can never remember, started laughing; another student wanted to see what he was looking at on his cell phone; someone else tried to get them to stop laughing; and, then, the fire alarm went off.

With various clauses filled with commas, the action in this sentence could easily become confusing. It helps to separate the key sections with semi-colons.

(3) Use a colon to introduce a list coming at the end of a sentence.

The writers learned about three key items in good fiction: plot, setting, and characterization.
Margie could cook three foods well: Ramen noodles, toast, and fried eggs.

(4) Use a colon to introduce an example or explanation.

There are only two ways to improve your writing skills: writing and writing some more.

(5) Use a colon to introduce an independent clause.

Whether or not to capitalize the first word following the colon is often a house style decision. *Chicago Manual of Style* says that if what follows the colon is a full sentence, then capitalize the first word.

For some people, Facebook is like a journal: They share every single emotion they feel at any given moment.

(6) Do not use a colon after *such as* or *including*.

Wrong: People too often abuse social media such as: Facebook, Instagram, and Snapchat.
Right: People too often abuse social media such as Facebook, Instagram, and Snapchat.

(7) Do not use a colon after a form of the verb *to be*.

Wrong: The three most popular forms of social media are: Facebook, Twitter, and Instagram.
Right: The three most popular forms of social media are Facebook, Twitter, and Instagram.

D. Quotation marks

(1) Punctuation generally goes inside quotation marks.

American usage does it this way; British puts the punctuation outside quotation marks. If you're writing for American publishers, do your quotation punctuating the American way.

Wrong: He answered, "For sure. We can use the compass to help guide us".
Right: He answered, "For sure. We can use the compass to help guide us."

Wrong: "Are you really going to carry your cell phone hiking"? she asked.
Right: "Are you really going to carry your cell phone hiking?" she asked.

(2) Punctuation goes outside the quotation marks if the punctuation is not part of the material in quotes.

Wrong: Who hasn't heard the song "Singin' in the Rain?"
Right: Who hasn't heard the song "Singin' in the Rain"?

The song title is correctly put in quotation marks. But the song title is not a question; that is, the title of the song is not "Singin' in the Rain?" But since this is a rhetorical question needing a question mark, the question mark goes outside the close quote.

Wrong: Remember Elton John's song "Can You Feel the Love Tonight?"?
Right: Remember Elton John's song "Can You Feel the Love Tonight?"

The song title is correctly put in quotation marks, but notice that this time the question mark *is* part of the song's title. Even though this is a question, you won't double up the question marks. This time the closing question mark goes inside the close quote and serves double duty.

Wrong: I enjoy playing Elton John's song "Can You Feel the Love Tonight?".

Wrong: I enjoy playing Elton John's song "Can You Feel the Love Tonight?."

Right: I enjoy playing Elton John's song "Can You Feel the Love Tonight?"

In this instance, this is a statement. The question mark stays inside the close quote as part of the song title, but don't then add a period either inside or outside the close quote.

(3) Don't put a close quotation mark at the end of a paragraph if the speaker continues into a new paragraph.

Wrong: "Blah blah blah."
"Blah blah blah blah. Now I'm done talking."
Right: "Blah blah blah.
"Blah blah blah blah. Now I'm done talking."

If you have a long-winded speaker in your book, and he goes on for paragraph after paragraph, don't put a close quote on his speech until he is completely finished. New paragraphs will begin with an open quote in his continuing monologue; close quote when he stops talking.

(4) Use single quotation marks for a quote within a quote.

Right: "Do you think I should say 'I'm sorry'?"
Right: Jay explained, "When Buddy opened the apartment door and saw everything covered in foil, he yelled, 'Hey! What's going on here?'"

E. "That" vs. "which"

Use "that" to introduce a restrictive (essential) clause that does not require commas; use "which" to introduce a nonessential clause that does require commas. Either is correct; it depends on the context.

Right: The manuscript that is due tomorrow is 175 pages.
Right: The manuscript, which is due tomorrow, is 175 pages.

F. "Who" vs. "whom"

When you're trying to decide whether to use "who" or "whom," ask yourself if the answer to the question would be "he" or "him." If "he" use "who"; if "him" use "whom."

I wonder (who, whom) will be at critique group today.

"He" will be at critique group.

"Him" will be at critique group.

Your answer to the question is that "he" will be at critique group. Therefore, the correct choice in the sample sentence is "I wonder <u>who</u> will be at critique group today."

(Who, Whom) are you going with?

I am going with "he."

I am going with "him."

Your answer is that you are going with "him." Therefore, the correct choice in the sample question is "Whom are you going with?"

One more note, please use *who* or *whom* for people, not *that*. For instance:

Wrong: The person <u>that</u> is first in line will win a free copy of the book.

Right: The person <u>who</u> is first in line will win a free copy of the book.

G. Hyphens vs. en-dashes vs. em-dashes

(1) Hyphens

Put a hyphen between compound modifiers that precede the word they modify:

Needs hyphen: Hayley is a part-time worker. ("Part-time" modifies "worker.")
No hyphen: Hayley works part time.

Needs hyphen: Jami is an out-of-state student. ("Out-of-state" modifies "student.")
No hyphen: Jami is from out of state.

Do not use hyphens with *–ly* adverbs:

Wrong: The Bible is a frequently-cited source.
Right: The Bible is a frequently cited source.

Wrong: Dr. Smith is a highly-esteemed professor at the university.
Right: Dr. Smith is a highly esteemed professor at the university.

Do not use hyphens after the words *less, least, many, most, very:*

Wrong: Sam is the least-educated man of the group.
Right: Sam is the least educated man of the group.

Wrong: Marian is the most-skillful tailor I've ever met.
Right: Marian is the most skillful tailor I've ever met.

If the first modifier modifies the second, use a hyphen.

Wrong: well respected speaker

Right: well-respected speaker ("Well" modifies not the speaker, but the word "respected")

(2) En-dash

Check the website for **Technical Tip: Inserting an En-dash.** Use an en-dash (–) for ranges of scores, dates, months, years:

Theirs was a May–December romance.

The score was 3–1 Colts.

We submitted chapters 10–12 on Tuesday.

Use an en-dash (–) to take the place of a hyphen if one of the modifiers is made up of two words.

The author was a Nobel Prize–winning physicist. ("Nobel Prize" is a two-word modifier, so use an en-dash after it and before "winning.")

He's a Des Moines–area native. ("Des Moines" is a two-word modifier for the word "area.")

(3) Em-dash

Often your Word program will default to an em-dash if you type your word, then two hyphens, then the following word (with no spaces around the hyphens). The two hyphens should automatically convert to an em-dash. Always remember that you do not put spacing around an em-dash; the words should butt up to it on both sides. If your program doesn't default to changing the two hyphens to an em-dash, check the website for **Technical Tip: Inserting an Em-dash.** Use an em-dash for emphasis or interruption. Be careful, however, not to overuse em-dashes. (This is something to check on those printed pages. You can easily see if you have too many. If so, replace some with other forms of punctuation.)

Writers like to attend writers conferences—especially the conferences that offer appointments with acquisitions editors and agents.

Few books published—less than one percent—become bestsellers.

H. Numbers

Chicago Manual of Style says to spell out numbers from one to one hundred, round numbers, and numbers at the beginning of sentences. See the following correct examples:

Thirty votes are needed, twenty-nine have been cast. I hope we get forty.

The property is held on a ninety-nine-year lease.

He wrote an essay of fifteen hundred words.

In books where you're following *Chicago Manual of Style*, use numerals for 101 and over (unless round numbers like "one million"), strings of numbers, and before the word "percent." See the following correct examples:

The first edition ran 2,670 pages in three volumes.

This is correct because the large number of pages is not a round number so is rendered in numerals. The word "three" is spelled out because numbers from one to one hundred are spelled out.

The ages of the students on the committee are 19, 20, and 22.

While numbers below one hundred are usually spelled out, that can begin to look awkward in strings of numbers. In the example above with the three sets of ages, it's cleaner and clearer to put in the numerals.

The experiment has a 43 percent chance of failing.

Using the numeral "43" is correct because numerals are always used with the word "percent." And remember that in nonscientific writing, use the word and not the symbol (%).

I. Time of day or night

Generally write out the time, unless the exact moment of time must be emphasized—then use numerals:

He left his office at quarter past six.

We always eat lunch at one o'clock.

Our favorite show comes on at 7:30 P.M.

We have to catch the 7:05 train.

Note that *Chicago Manual of Style* prefers small caps with periods— A.M. or P.M. Publishers have their own preferences. You might use p.m. or PM. If you want small caps, do lower case "p.m." and then highlight the letters. Press Control + Shift + K to get small caps. Whichever way you choose, be consistent throughout the manuscript.

J. Italics

Wondering whether something should be italicized or put in quotation marks? Here's an easy way to remember: The larger work is in italics; the portion of the larger work is in quotation marks. For example, use italics for book titles but quotation marks for chapter titles; use italics for a magazine title but quotation marks for an article title; use italics for a newspaper name but quotation marks for the title of an article. Play names, television shows, and movie titles are italicized.

I read the chapter "Writing Strong Characters" in the book *How to Write Your Novel.*

My article titled, "Where Your Taxes Go" was on the front page of *The New York Times*.

We watched *Iron Man* for the fourth time, after watching *Thor*.

Use italics for foreign phrases.

I tried it and *voilà!* It worked!

I asked, and the waiter pointed me to the door marked *baño*.

Use italics for sounds as sounds.

I squeezed the balloon and *pop!* It broke.

We all jumped when a loud *boom* blasted through the office.

K. Ellipses

If you're going to use ellipses, either use the "..." that automatically appears in your word processing program, or type each dot with a space between. Choose one method and use it consistently throughout the manuscript. Remember: Three dots for a break; four dots if the previous sentence is a complete sentence (because the first dot is the period).

"The fruit of the Spirit is ... patience."

"In the beginning God created the heavens and the earth. ... And he saw that it was good."

Creating Your Personal Style Sheet

A style sheet will help you as you copyedit yourself, someone else who does a copyedit pass for you, and ultimately, the copy editor at your publishing house if your book gets that far. Want your copy editor to send you chocolates (or flowers)? Include a style sheet. (I can't promise the chocolates or flowers, but you will be well loved, I promise.)

While copy editors will follow the rules of the style manuals for their industry and the style guides for their publishing house, they also know that each project (especially in books) will often need its own style sheet, and they will create one if you don't.

On these style sheets, explain exceptions to "the rules." Such as these that I included on recent style sheets I've created for projects:

- Author wants to capitalize "Heaven" throughout.

- Author wants to use his own version of Bible book abbreviations (list attached).

- Author wants to use a period at the end of a subhead if the subhead creates a sentence.

- Author is purposely using British spellings on certain words.

- Author wants to lower case certain proper nouns (list attached).

If you have particular ways you want to treat some words, or certain style elements you want to use for your manuscript, make a list of those items and keep it with your manuscript. Then, if you hire a copy editor, or if the manuscript makes its way to an agent or acquisitions editor, they won't be confused and they won't undo what you've done because it's "incorrect." They will understand your reasoning behind those choices.

You know your manuscript better than anyone, and you know the decisions you've made along the way and why. Even if you're not under contract and need to explain yourself to an editor, it helps to keep a style sheet *for your information.* Keep track of anything unusual that you do—capping or lowercasing certain words and unusual spellings of words (include a word list), whether you decided to upper case or lower case deity pronouns (so you'll be consistent throughout), and anything else you might consider particular to your manuscript.

I realize that you might feel a bit overwhelmed—grammar rules have a way of doing that. Do your best. Following these grammar rules (or knowing why you're breaking them) goes a long way to creating a clean, readable, marketable manuscript. Let's move on to some final touches that will polish your manuscript.

6
Copyediting:
Making Final Touches

After you have completed the more mechanical work of fixing grammar and punctuation, it's time to talk about some of the other details that will help your manuscript shine—proving to your first readers that you have gone over and above in your care for the quality of your manuscript. In this chapter, I'll address some of those details, from common problems at the word and sentence level, "Christianese," and obtaining permissions for quoted material.

You may be saying to yourself, "I have to read my manuscript *again?*" I feel your pain. I've gotten to the point in my writing that I don't think I can read my words one more time. I'll repeat that this is why it's vital to take time with your manuscript and to take breaks between these various phases of self-editing. You can't do everything in one pass—your brain won't let you. So after you've fixed all the grammar issues, let the manuscript sit for a week or so, then go back and consider the following.

Study Your Words

Focus on *every single word.* Make every word promise that it's there for a reason. Make sure every word is the *best* word for what you're trying to say. Consider your adjectives:

- Is *shiny* the best word, or should it be *glossy, gleaming, sparkly, glittery, polished, shimmering, glistening, burnished, reflective?*
- Is *cloudy* the best word, or is *overcast, gloomy,* or *hazy* better?

- Is *sad* the best word, or should it be *unhappy, miserable, depressed, gloomy, down, blue, wretched, dejected, despondent, desolate, forlorn, sorrowful, melancholy, woeful?*

- Is *happy* the best word, or should it be *content, pleased, glad, joyful, cheerful, blissful, exultant, ecstatic, delighted, cheery, jovial, in high spirits?*

Microsoft Word has both a dictionary and a thesaurus to help you. Click on the "Review" tab, and on the left is a "Define" button. Click on the word you want to define, then click the define button. A window will open up on the right with a definition. There is also a "Thesaurus" button. Highlight a word and click on it; a window on the right will offer you several synonyms (and even a few antonyms) to help you out. On a Mac, you will find "Smart Lookup," which will explore or define; push "Thesaurus" to get synonyms and antonyms.

Revise generic words for specific words. Specifics help to create a strong setting and tell your readers much about your characters. Consider what you learn about the characters when you take a generic word and add detail. For example: Don't say that your character drives a "car." Say instead that he drives a beat-up mini-van, or a 1967 Corvette convertible, or a Bentley.

The details give us particular impressions. You don't have to tell us your character is wealthy if you tell us what he drives or where he lives or how he dresses. You can also use the details to surprise your readers. Maybe your rich elderly man doesn't drive a Bentley; maybe he drives a beat-up mini-van. That tells us something about him. These kinds of details allow you to drop information about your characters in various places throughout the manuscript without having to do what Maxwell Perkins called an "information dump."

As you reread your manuscript, take note of what you as author see as you read. For example, the woman opens her "purse." When you read the word *purse* in the context of your manuscript, what do you see? Leather and fringe? A massive designer bag? A clutch? A bag covered in sequins with unicorns? Then revise "purse" to describe exactly what you see.

Consider the verbs. Even if you got rid of many of the pesky *–ly* adverbs for stronger verbs in your earlier self-editing pass, sometimes the verbs still need polishing. Don't say your character "walked" if in your mind you see her jogging or ambling or limping or scurrying or tip-toeing.

The strong verbs tell us much about the situation. You don't have to tell us she's in a hurry or scared or hurt if you use verbs that make it clear.

Study Your Sentences

Sentence fragments

A sentence fragment is a sentence that doesn't have a subject and a verb.

> *Incorrect:* Sometimes writers claim to experience writer's block. <u>No such thing</u>.
> *Correct:* Sometimes writers claim to experience writer's block, although many other writers say there is no such thing.

While the first example is technically incorrect because of the fragment, "No such thing," note that sentence fragments aren't always wrong. Your style may be that you sometimes write in fragments. Like this. Make sure that if you have a fragment, you're doing it on purpose, and make sure that it is appropriate for what you're writing.

Run-on sentences

Sometimes you get so excited in your writing that you just keep on writing and writing, forgetting to put in punctuation writing as if you can't seem to stop your thoughts from going and going because you're trying to keep up with your racing mind. ... See? These run-on sentences are easy to notice if you read your manuscript aloud. If you run out of breath, you're probably running on. Go back and punctuate those sentences properly.

> *Incorrect:* The math test was planned for Monday, October 2, but several of the students who were in an art class had a field trip to the Indianapolis Art Museum in Indianapolis and it was going to be an all-day excursion, so the professor rescheduled the test for the following Friday, when all the students would be in class.

Better: The math test, which had been planned for Monday, October 2, was rescheduled for the following Friday to accommodate the students who were required to attend that Monday's all-day art class field trip to the Indianapolis Art Museum.

Misplaced or dangling modifiers

A *misplaced modifier* occurs when the modifier in a sentence is in the wrong spot, modifying a word it shouldn't modify. This can create a confusing, if not hilarious, scenario.

Incorrect: Hanging from the cave ceiling, the spelunker took a picture of the bats.

The way this is written, it sounds like the spelunker is hanging from the ceiling. While that may be the case (depending on context and this particular spelunker), most likely the scenario is that he took a picture of the bats that were hanging from the ceiling. So revise this to say:

Better: The spelunker took a picture of the bats hanging from the cave ceiling.

A *dangling modifier* occurs when there is no object being modified. My sister just told me about her daughter's graduation ceremony this past week. As speakers on the platform called the names and handed out diplomas, a student left the platform and discovered she had a diploma with someone else's name on it. The platform speakers paused the ceremony for several minutes to sort out the problem. After a few minutes, the ceremony continued. One might say:

Incorrect: With a sigh of relief, the ceremony continued.

However, a ceremony can't sigh. Here's what actually happened:

Correct: With a sigh of relief, the speakers on the platform continued the ceremony.

Fix misplaced or dangling modifiers by rearranging or adding words.

Parallelism

Elements in your sentences need to be parallel. See the following sentences for what I mean.

Incorrect: The candidate's goals include winning the election, a revised tax code, and the educational system.

Better: The candidate's goals include winning the election, revising the tax code, and reforming the educational system.

The second sentence reads better because of the parallel *–ing* words: winning, revising, reforming.

Unclear pronoun references

Watch your sentences for clarity with pronouns and make sure that the references you make go along with the closest pronoun. For example, here's a sentence that, while grammatically correct, includes an unclear pronoun reference:

Incorrect: When she was thirty, Andrea's mother died.

Did Andrea's mother die when she was age thirty, or did Andrea's mother die when Andrea was age thirty? The sentence could be taken either way. So change it to say exactly what you mean. Here are a couple ways to do it:

Correct: When Andrea turned thirty, her mother died.

Correct: Andrea was just a child when her thirty-year-old mother died.

Here's another example

Incorrect: Three bicycles were reported stolen by the police yesterday.

This sounds like someone reported that police are stealing bicycles. Well, maybe, it depends on what's going on in your story. Chances are, however, that the sentence should be recast.

Correct: Yesterday, the police reported that thieves stole three bicycles from in front of the mini-mart.

I found the following error in a Bible revision I was editing:

Incorrect: When the Israelites woke up the next morning, they were all dead.

Who was dead? The Israelites couldn't have been dead since they "woke up." Obviously, the word *they* was referring to someone in a previous sentence. This error occurred in the story in 2 Chronicles 32 when the Lord sent an angel to cut down the Assyrian army that had surrounded Jerusalem. Thus:

Correct: When the Israelites woke up the next morning, <u>every soldier in the entire Assyrian army</u> was dead.

Active vs. passive voice

While it isn't grammatically incorrect, passive voice signifies lazy writing. You can identify passive voice if you see many forms of the verb "to be." Advice recently bouncing around my editing friends' Facebook posts says, "If you can add 'by zombies' to the end of your sentence, the sentence is in passive voice." Thus:

Passive voice: The food was eaten.

Can I add "by zombies" and have the sentence make sense? Yes. "The food was eaten by zombies." In this case, however, I want to make the point that the food was eaten by the college students. Again, the fact that I need the word *by* signifies that I am writing in passive voice. Also, notice the form of the "to be" verb: *was*. You change from passive voice to active voice by making the subject of your sentence do the action. Who ate the food?

Active voice: The college students ate every last morsel of food on the buffet.

Here's another example:

Passive voice: Mike was attacked in his own front yard by the neighbor's pit bull.

Notice the word *by*, and a form of the "to be" verb: *was*. Revise this to active voice:

Active voice: The neighbor's pit bull attacked Mike in his own front yard.

You don't have to eliminate every instance of passive voice because sometimes it works for the context. However, make sure that when you use it, you use it strategically. Don't let your writing come across as lazy. Be specific and precise.

The problem of he/she

Increasingly, I'm seeing writers employ the third-person plural with a singular antecedent to avoid the problem of having to choose a masculine or feminine pronoun. For example:

Each individual must decide about their faith.

This is technically incorrect because the plural pronoun *their* doesn't match with the singular noun *individual*. Some will write this way, using one pronoun to stand for everyone:

Each individual must decide about his faith. OR
Each individual must decide about her faith.

These sentences sound like you're ignoring one gender or the other. You do have several other options, such as:

Each individual must decide about his or her faith.

That is fine and grammatically correct, but too many of these types of sentences will become cumbersome for the reader. Your other option is to recast your sentences in the plural:

All people must make individual decisions about their faith.

That, too, is grammatically correct.

My best advice is to consider your context. If you're a mom writing a book about mothering to an audience of moms, use the feminine pronoun most of the time—even if a few dads out there will read the book for advice because they are in that role. I honestly don't think any of them will be offended.

If it's important to you to be inclusive, use the plural as much as sounds natural. Another option is to just go back and forth with a few sentences using the masculine, others using the feminine.

Deity pronouns (capitalize or not?)

It used to be fairly standard for third-person pronouns referring to God, Jesus, and the Holy Spirit to be capitalized—He, Him, His, Himself, etc. Sometimes even the second-person pronouns referring to God are also capitalized—"We love You, Lord."

This is a decision based on your preferences. As you're writing, be consistent. Some publishing houses go one way or another, so if your manuscript gets picked up, you may be asked to change the capitalization to their style. If you feel strongly one way or the other, this is a decision you can add to your style sheet that you created to go with your manuscript.

If you're quoting from Scripture, however, you must quote exactly, even if it's different from your treatment of deity pronouns in the rest of your manuscript. For example, some Bible versions, such as the New King James Version, capitalize the deity pronouns; in various other versions (KJV, NLT, NIV, for example), the deity pronouns are not capitalized. If you decide that in your writing you want to capitalize deity pronouns, but you're quoting from a Bible version that does not, you still need to quote verses exactly as the Bible version has it, even if it is inconsistent with your writing.

Avoiding "Christianese"

Every group has its own "language"—the terminology of people who are in the military or work in a particular industry, build computers and write code, or even work in a kitchen as chefs. Those of us not privy to the meanings behind some terms or the names for some pieces of equipment or even the acronyms associated with a particular business will find ourselves at a loss. Help any "outsiders" with the insiders' lingo as you write.

Christians certainly have our own language filled with words that we understand but might mean nothing to those who haven't grown up in the church. The Evangelical Publishers Association prints this on its website:

> "Christianese" is a language used in the Christian subculture and understood easily only by other practicing Christians. We say we've been born again, or talk about being backslidden. We talk about our walk and our quiet time. When you're talking about the Christian experience, it's tempting to slip into Christianese—it's a language with verbal short-cuts to explain some difficult concepts. But if our hope is to communicate effectively with people outside the Christian community, we want to stay away from clichés and figures of speech that they may not understand, or may understand differently than we do.

> It's also good to avoid Christianese when we're aiming our message at a Christian audience—especially if our goal is to lead them to fresh encounters with biblical truth. For the Christian reader, Christianese has very

little impact. We've heard the words again and again, and the result is that we don't really pay attention to what they signify.[17]

As a believer writing for either a Christian or non-Christian audience, it's vital that you be cognizant and careful about terms that are specific to Christians but might have no meaning to nonbelievers or terms that, because of overuse, might have lost their meaning for believers. When it comes to writing about faith, don't assume that just because it's about God it will be great. In fact, as Christian writers, it's even more important for us to strive to write in a way that honors God—doing all the hard work that it takes to use a gift well, and in this case, the gift of writing.

The EPA website quoted above has a list of terms to avoid. These include:

backsliding

born again

fruit of the Spirit

Jesus in my heart

salvation

sanctified

sin

Get the picture? These are all terms that mean something to Christians; however, to someone not churched or people discovering faith for the first time, these words can be confusing. It can sound like we're speaking our own language, some sort of insider code from which our readers are excluded. In an article titled, "How NOT to Speak Christianese," Luke Cawley explains it this way:

If you don't believe me, try this experiment: Think about the word "conversion." It is filled with meaning for you, from all the Bible studies, books, and talks you have absorbed. If you had never encountered the Christian faith, though, what imagery would "conversion" trigger in your mind? Take 20 seconds to see what comes to mind.

I usually hear it used to describe a building project that makes the attic habitable (a "loft conversion"), as a term for comparing the relative value of money from different countries (a "currency conversion"), or as a way of changing the format of a document on a computer ("file conversion in progress").

Sometimes I hear it described in relation to religion. But, with a few possible exceptions, religious conversion in our culture is not viewed warmly or perceived as an inviting prospect for most people. In fact, it often has overtones of manipulation ("that person is trying to convert me") or of desperation (as in "deathbed conversion").

"Conversion," then, is not the straightforward word for most people that it is for Christians.[18]

As Christian writers, writing our faith doesn't mean we have to write about God at every turn. Instead, as believers, everything we write will be infused with our faith, as it should be. Yet it's our challenge as Christian writers who have the best message in the world—no matter whether we're writing fiction books or nonfiction books or articles or devotionals—to speak in a language that our readers will understand. Let's not be obtuse by being lazy with our words. Let's look for the words that will speak to our audience, words that will help open to them the world of our faith and invite them in.

Obtaining Permissions

When do you need to get permission to quote from another source? This is an important question—and getting it wrong can be problematic (and may be very expensive). An editor at a publisher will spot when you need permission and require that you do the footwork to get it. When you do said footwork, you may find that the publisher of the work from which you want to quote wants so much money that you decide maybe you don't need that quote after all.

So let's talk about the when and how of obtaining permissions.

First, realize that whenever you use someone else's creative material, you need permission. Just apply the "do unto others" rule. Suppose you write a book that took you several years and tons of research. Then along comes someone else who loved your book and quotes several paragraphs from it—that person then also selling a book and making money technically from some of your hard-won research. It's only fair that you should be compensated (if even in a small way) for that person's usage of your material. United States copyright law protects creative material from misuse and generally requires asking for permission.

Even if you're self-publishing and thinking no one will ever see your little book, don't short-cut this process. You never know what will happen. Your book could take off and then, suddenly, the fact that you neglected to request permission for quoted work will suddenly become an issue and may end up costing you in legal fees everything you make in the book's sales. It's simply not worth it.

However, because of the type of information requested by a publisher, there is no reason to write to a publisher to request permission to quote material until you are under contract or if you're planning to self-publish. After you read the type of information that publishers request and understand that most will require a fee for quoted material, think carefully about how much you want to lean on other people's material in your book.

You will be requesting permission from the copyright holder of each work. Generally, if the work is still in print, the process is to write to the publisher, which has been simplified immensely in the past few years with most permissions able to be requested online at a publisher's website. If the rights have reverted to the author, then you will need to locate that author and request permission. Below, I show you a sample of the types of information I would need to give a publisher if I were to request to quote material from one of that publisher's books. Include all of this in a letter to the copyright holder if you need to contact an individual as opposed to a publisher.

Be organized before you begin. For example, if I wanted to quote a paragraph or more from *Confessions of a Comma Queen,* by Mary Norris (a great little book, by the way), I need to go to the publisher's website, W. W. Norton and navigate around to try to find a tab for "Permissions." Most of the time you'll find it buried in a publisher's Contact page, or you might find it in small print in the footer of the publisher's web pages. At the W. W. Norton website, I have to go to the bottom footer, locate the tiny "Contact" button, click on that, and then choose "Permissions" from the options. I then received a form to fill in electronically.

First, the form wants my personal information. Then, it needs the information about the book I'm quoting from (so I have to have it in front of me). In this case, I needed:

- Author
- ISBN [*on the bar code on the back as well as on the copyright page*]
- Copyright line [*from the copyright page*]
- Page(s) [*where the quote I want is located*]
- Title of selection [*if what I want to quote has a section title*]
- Total number of pages [*that comprise my quote—if it is a paragraph that goes from one page to another, then two pages*]
- Total word count of the quote I want to use
- Total number of lines of my quote [*lines from the original book*]
- Total number of illustration(s) [*in my case, none, but if you were using a photo or a chart, this information is required*]

But wait, I'm only partway there. Next, I have to talk about *my* book. Since this book is under contract, I would need to ask my publisher, Bold Vision Books, for some of this information as I begin the process of requesting permission.

- Title of my book
- Author/Editor
- Publisher
- Publication date

- Publication format (options include hardcover, paperback, e-book, website, audio CD, CD-ROM/DVD, Musical setting, other) [*I can click as many as apply*]

- Number of pages [*referring to total number of pages in my book—this page count makes sure that what I'm quoting does not comprise too much of a percentage of my total book*]

- Total Print Run/Total Quantity [*I would ask Bold Vision Books for the number of how many books will be in the first print run*]

- Price

- Territory (options include North America, Worldwide, Other) [*Again, I would double-check with Bold Vision Books or see if it's clear in my contract*]

- Then there's a box for additional comments

Seeking written permission is a process to do once you're under contract so that you have the required information from your publisher. If you're self-publishing, pull everything together and explain what you can't in the comments box. Try to pursue permissions as early as possible; don't wait until the last minute. Try to give publishers from one to three months to get back to you. If a publisher doesn't get back to you, you'll need to take out the quoted material. If the publisher writes back and wants money for the quote, you decide if the quote is worth paying for. If not, then rewrite those sections and remove any references to the quoted material.

The publisher will expect you to pay for the permissions out of your advance. My contract stipulates that I as author will obtain the permissions, send copies of all permission letters to Bold Vision prior to the release of the work, and pay any fees related to permissions. This contract clause is standard.

That's the *how* of obtaining permission. Now for *when* you need to seek permission to quote.

If you're quoting from works dated prior to 1923, the U.S. Copyright Office says that they are in the public domain. For example, the words of many of the old hymns are in the public domain. Classic works are in the public domain. But realize that a version of a book published before 1923, such as an updated classic published recently, is *not* in the public domain. That updated book has a copyright held by that publisher. The only version of a work still in public domain would be the actual book with a date on its copyright page prior to 1923.

Recent rulings have determined that for works published since 1978, copyright protection lasts for seventy years past the death of the author. For works before 1978 by a single author, the copyright protection is ninety-five years from the date of publication. Thus, not all "old" works are out of copyright and in the public domain.

See how confusing this becomes? Read the copyright law (I did, pages and pages online), and you'll only end up more confused. And if you read examples of copyright cases that ended up in court, it gets even worse. The subjectivity leaves cases open to the whim of a judge or jury.

The term "fair use" means that writers can freely use small portions of printed works. But this terminology is extremely tricky and subjective, and fair use laws are not clear. Here's the gist: You can use copyrighted material for what copyright law calls "limited and transformative" purposes—to comment upon or criticize (such as in a book review), or even as a parody—and this kind of quoting can be done without requesting permission. However, be aware that lawsuits get filed all the time over this issue, and without hard and fast rules, judges decide cases based on a variety of factors, such as how you used the material, the nature of the original work, how much and how substantial was the portion you quoted, and the effect of your use on the potential market.

My best advice to you? If you're quoting a single line or a few lines from a book and giving full credit for it, you're probably okay under fair use law. You'll hear or read a lot of different pieces of advice about how many words are "safe" to quote, but again, the terms are a gray area. No one has ever made a law or rule saying "under X number of words" is fair use—precisely because of the other factors noted above, such as intent, and substantiality, percentage of the full work, etc.

If you're quoting a single line from a novel, and saying the title of the novel and the author (that is, you're not plagiarizing by trying to pass it off as your own—another issue entirely), then you are probably fine under fair use. However, realize that a single line from a poem or from a song constitutes a much higher percentage of that original piece and is not considered fair use. Music lyrics are extremely problematic.

The music industry has developed strict rules about the use of song lyrics—often asking not only an upfront fee, but also a portion on the royalties for every book sold that includes the line with lyric. You as author most likely will not want to pay the upfront cost to use the lyrics (which can run into hundreds or thousands of dollars); most publishers are not interested in dealing with the complexity of figuring royalty payments that way. My best advice is to remove lyrics entirely to save everyone the hassle.

I recently copyedited a book in which the author did a pilgrimage along the Camino de Santiago, a pilgrimage route from the Middle Ages that stretches five hundred miles across northern Spain. He often sang to himself as he walked, and he included the lyrics to those songs in his book. While the lyrics often supplied insight into his thoughts and feelings during his pilgrimage (which is why he included them), we as his editors knew he would run into permissions problems. He reluctantly removed the song lyrics.

Every case is subjective. Don't think that just because you said where the quote came from that you're covered. It's better to be safe than sorry. But being overly cautious could cause you to pay for quotes that would technically be fair use. However, if you start quoting several sentences or paragraphs or using data or using photos or tables, get thee to the permissions page of the publisher's website and ask. It's far better to request permission and cover yourself, and far better to pay the fee to use that person's creative material or drop that other person's material from your book entirely than to leave it in and experience the expense of a lawsuit.

This finishes your copyediting process. Let's move on to proofreading.

7
Proofreading:
One Last Pass

At this phase of your project, the content editing has organized and checked the entire arc of your book, and the copyedit has formatted your manuscript, clarified your sentences, and fixed your grammar and punctuation. Now you're doing a final pass, called a *proofread*. In this chapter, we'll consider what makes proofreading different from copyediting, and then we'll talk about what to look for in your proofread.

Copyediting vs. Proofreading

Copyediting is examining the sentences and the words, and correcting grammar, punctuation, and spelling. The point is to do such a good job at that level that the pages are pristine. This step is where the rubber meets the road (to use an overused cliché). Copyediting puts your best foot forward (to use another overused cliché—which is the "best foot" anyway?). When this manuscript arrives on the desk of the AE or the agent or the editor, believe me, you don't want the reader getting so distracted by errors that he or she can't focus on your brilliant writing. So that's why you must do the next step, which is to proofread.

Trust me. I've seen a few of unprofessional manuscripts. Perhaps the formatting was off (hello? You're sending me a hundred pages of single-spaced copy? In a weird, impossible-to-read font?). Besides formatting issues, I've also seen pages so riddled with mistakes that I couldn't get past the distracting errors to understand what the author was trying to say.

You must proofread before sending your manuscript into the world.

Proofreading Process

Again, let the manuscript sit for a few days or longer. You are so close to the manuscript that you can easily overlook your mistakes. Then begin.

Start electronically. The word processing program has a spelling checker that will give you squiggly lines under words that might be spelled incorrectly or phrases that the program thinks are somehow wrong. But don't depend on it being always correct, and don't use it exclusively. The spelling checker is not going to catch words spelled correctly but used incorrectly, for example. Some of the later versions of Word attempt to pick up grammar nuances. It's worth checking the marked items, but don't assume that Word is either correct or incorrect. And don't assume that the items marked are all you need to check. You must still read the entire manuscript.

Do a search for an open parenthesis (to make sure that you always have a matching close parenthesis), an open quotation mark (to make sure you always have the appropriate closing quotation mark and to make sure any inner quotation marks are single and that both are there). At this point, make sure that the punctuation surrounding your quotation marks is rendered correctly.

If you know you have a tendency to overuse certain words, phrases, or punctuation marks (hello exclamation points!), go on a search and destroy mission. It is easy to do by searching through your electronic document. For example, I mentioned my tendency to constantly use the word *so*, especially at the beginning of sentences. It's a habit. *So* I did a search and removed it everywhere that it was a wasted word. My editor noted that I constantly repeated the phrases "you can" or "you will need to" or "you will want to." She said, "Just tell the reader to do it, not that they 'will want to' do it." Again, the computer came to the rescue. My eyes weren't going to catch that on the hard copy—it's just natural for me to write that way. But when I searched for those phrases, it showed me how I did indeed constantly use them, And it showed me *all* of them, allowing me to remove the places where these were wasted words.

Now that I know this about myself, I will check for these problems in everything I write in the future. Be aware of your weaknesses. If you know that possessives always mess you up, do a search for apostrophes and check each one for correct usage.

After you've let the computer tell you as much as it can, print a copy of your manuscript and get to work with a red or blue pen (black is the same as your font color and might be too easy to miss as you make corrections. And, yes, your purple pen is fine, too). I can't stress enough that proofreading on hard copy will offer a better visual on the pages than you get from your computer screen.

Scribble all over your manuscript. Read slowly and carefully. Look at each word. Watch for details such as a missing period, a comma that should be a semi-colon, a semi-colon that should be a colon, transposed letters, missing apostrophes, hyphens that should be em-dashes (- vs. —), missing open or close quotation marks, missing open or close parentheses, etc.

And, of course, keep an eye out for word- and sentence-level problems, including grammar, spelling, punctuation, dangling modifiers, run-on sentences—everything we discussed during the copyediting process that you might have missed. Again, be aware of your weaknesses. If you know you tend to write run-on sentences, watch for them. If you know your modifiers often dangle or that you tend to leave unclear antecedents, keep an eye out.

Use a dictionary. If a word suddenly stops you—say, you're just not sure if *ameba* is spelled that way or should be *amoeba* or *ameoba*—look it up.

Read aloud slowly to yourself. Reading aloud will help you notice if words are missing or if a sentence runs on and on. Then, read it again starting from the bottom paragraph backward, a paragraph at a time. This reverse reading helps you get outside your flow and see errors you might skip over otherwise.

Proofreading Checklist

Following are a few other items to check during your proofread.

✔ Spellings of proper names and unfamiliar words. (Is that ubiquitous store WalMart or Wal-Mart or Wal-mart or Walmart? It's the last one. Double check your spelling of

Azerbaijan. Make sure that King Jehoshaphat has all the letter h's it needs.)

✔ Extra spaces between words and sentences.

✔ Extra punctuation (such as a double period).

✔ Bolds and italics—are they on the words you want bolded or italicized?

✔ Correct editorial style according to the publisher style guides—deity caps, serial commas, capitalizations, Bible book abbreviations, etc., or according to your own style sheet if you don't have a publisher yet.

✔ Correspondence between footnote or endnote numbers in the text and the entries in the footnotes or endnotes.

✔ Correspondence between notes and bibliography.

✔ Correct rendering of footnotes and endnotes (first line indent on footnotes and endnotes; hanging indent on bibliography entries).

✔ Table of contents titles match the titles at the beginning of the chapters.

✔ "Curly" quotes, not straight or smart quotes, on quotation marks and apostrophes.

✔ Double check any copy that is ALL CAPS (such as in titles, etc.). It is easy to overlook misspellings in copy that is ALL CAPS.

✔ Consistency in all of your features. If you start every chapter halfway down the page, with "Chapter" then number, and then the chapter title in all caps—make sure that you do exactly the same at the beginning of every chapter.

Let me reiterate that while you can do your best, it's advisable to get another set of eyes on your book. Pay a professional proofreader to go through all of the above steps. Final proofreading is extremely important because it is the final piece of the puzzle. The proofread manuscript is what the agent or AE sees.

After you've finished with the proofreading on the printed copy, go into the electronic document and incorporate all of the changes. Save the clean copy as your "final" version on your computer so you always know which one is the most perfect one. This new document with all the corrections is the manuscript that will be sent off to your agent or the one that goes to the publisher in accordance with your contract.

I can guarantee you that people all down the line who read your manuscript or the typeset pages will still find typos. In fact, when your book arrives in all its printed glory, somewhere a typo will rear its ugly head. Them's the breaks. I'm already steeling myself for finding a typo in this chapter on proofreading. It happens. You're human; we're all human. Even the best proofreaders miss errors.

We do the best we can. But the fact that you're reading this book and learning the steps? Your manuscript will have a far better chance of being the clean manuscript AEs and agents love to receive.

Now let's make sure that, if you quote or refer to the Bible in your manuscript, that you take care to handle it correctly.

8
Working with Bible Text

Writers who write for Christian publishing often quote Scripture. These quotes appear more in the nonfiction world than in the fiction world. (In fiction, if your character butchers quoting a Bible verse, for example, maybe that's just part of his charm.) However, in nonfiction books, quotations are used as source material, as part of a study, or part of a devotional. Quoting Scripture is important and quoting it *correctly* is of supreme importance.

The Bible is God's Word, and we want to follow Paul's advice to Timothy: "Do your best to present yourself to God as one approved, a worker who does not need to be ashamed and who *correctly handles the word of truth*" (2 Timothy 2:15 NIV, italics mine). The Word of God serves as our proof text, our foundation, and our source of deep study and inspiration. We must *know* it well, implying that, as Christian writers, we're in the Word daily. We want to be careful not to misquote, not to misuse, not to make the Bible say something it doesn't. We need to know it in context. I spent my editing lifetime in Christian publishing and have done my share of work with Bible text.

"I Edit the Bible"

Back in the late 1980s, I was involved in a huge Bible project that was a partnership between Tyndale House Publishers and Youth for Christ to create a brand-new kind of study Bible. Our purpose in *The Life Application Study Bible* was to go beyond what most study Bibles of the day were doing, which was to offer a lot of information but little insight. We wanted to create a Bible that gave information and insight but then also took the person to the "so what?" question. We wanted to help Bible readers understand what various verses and passages mean for daily living.

The partnership with Tyndale was marrying Ken Taylor's *Living Bible* text (his massively popular paraphrase from the 1970s that made the Bible readable for people of average reading level) with our vision for Bible notes (which would do the same). We wanted to make sure every note guided the reader to answer the question personally, "I just read this in Scripture. So what? What does that mean for *my* life?"

A team of us at YFC began work. We all kept our regular day jobs, but each day set several hours aside and gathered around the big rectangular table in the office conference room. We stayed late, sometimes coming in on Saturdays. One person read the next day's passage and targeted where we would need notes. With the conference room table piled high with commentaries and Bible dictionaries, we worked on the targeted passages of Scripture by diving into those resources and reading what the great evangelicals had written. The discussions focused on attempting to write an understandable note that clarified difficulties and knotty theological issues, and also answered the "so what?" question. I sat at the head of the conference table, jotting on note cards trying to capture their discussion (gosh, a laptop would have been nice!). When finished, I read the note back to the group, and we'd edit until it felt right. Then, I set the card aside, pulled up a new one, and we'd move to the next targeted verse or passage.

After each of our marathon sessions, I took my pile of scribbled, crossed out, and re-scribbled notecards and typed the contents into the brand-new computer purchased for our office just for this purpose. It had a black screen with orange lettering and an annoying blinking orange rectangle for a cursor. I entered the notes in canonical order and then printed each Bible book's material out on the wide paper with the holes on each side—the obnoxious holes that wouldn't always stay on their little spindles as the paper jerked through the printer line by line, often jamming. These hard copies then went through a series of editorial passes, then came back to me to enter changes. Sometimes an edit would be far down in the file, so I'd hit search and then go get a cup of coffee. By the time I got back, the "search" mode might have found the note I wanted.

This process went on for a couple of busy years. In the end, we came up with an amazing product—totally and completely new in the marketplace, something never seen before. After the complete *Life Application Study Bible* in The Living Bible paraphrase came out around 1988, I worked as a freelancer on the LAB by revising every ancillary feature to match seven different Bible versions (we began in *The Living Bible,* then did the King James Version, the New King James Version, Revised Standard Version, New Revised Standard Version, New International Version, New American Standard, Holman Christian Standard). Seven years, approximately a translation a year. The life application concept was such a massive success and such a new approach to a study Bible that every publisher wanted it. (In the world of Bible publishing, there are public domain texts, such as some versions of the King James Version, and then pretty much every heavy-hitting Bible publisher owns its own—pays to have it created or purchases one. That way, they can create various kinds of study and devotional Bibles without having to pay royalties to another publisher to use their Bible text.) Those publishers wanted to be able to sell the LAB in their own translation.

What that meant was that *someone* needed to go through all of the ancillary material and make it match the wording of the new Bible version text. That someone was me.

During those seven years, I would receive the default original version of all the Bible notes and features (map copy, chart copy, people profile notes, book introductions) and a Bible (not electronic, just a book) with the new version. The notes came to me on 5-1/4-inch floppy disks. I would insert the disk in my computer, open Genesis and begin to work first on the Bible book intro. Wherever we quoted Scripture, I had to look it up and revise it match the new version. At times, place names or people names would be treated differently: Is Saul's son named Ishbosheth or Ish-bosheth or Ish-Bosheth or Ish Bosheth (it's actually all of them, depending on which Bible version). Eventually I learned to watch for key words that might be different (NIV says the Israelites wandered in the "desert"; most other versions say "wilderness"). Some versions have John the Baptist's mother spelled with a z "Elizabeth," some with an s "Elisabeth"; some have his father as Zechariah and some as Zacharias. In some, Esther is married to King Ahasuerus; in others, King Xerxes. These differences are not an issue of error; it's an issue of translation and sources and Greek and Hebrew—and I suppose, whatever the translation committee eventually agreed upon. And then, of course, some versions use uppercase deity pronouns (such as the NKJV) and some do not. For those that did, every reference to God or Jesus or the Holy Spirit as a he or a him or a himself or a his in the ancillary material had to be tracked down and fixed with a capital H.

Suffice it to say, I've been around the Bible for a bit. If there's anything I know, it's working with the Bible text. I'm no expert by a long shot. I still depend on people who have degrees in theology or Bible to help me sort through a thorny issue in a manuscript. If you're writing for a publisher with a particular denominational leaning, know the nuances of its theology. But the years of exposure to Scripture have given me a basic understanding and a more sensitive radar to writing that might be a bit "off."

Rules and Advice for Quoting and Sourcing Scripture

You already learned about how to source your Bible material on the copyright page; it will be easier to build that material if you've been careful to do that sourcing on the Bible text throughout your manuscript.

You may decide that you will quote just from one version of Scripture, or you may want to use a variety. Many versions read differently, and you may discover that one version reads in such a way that you want to quote that one. Just be sure to give the required information.

If you're quoting from only one version throughout the manuscript, you don't need to give the Bible version after all of the references. Your line on the copyright page stating that "All Scripture quotations are taken from ..." is sufficient. However, if you at one point decide to quote from another version—say just one verse—on *that* verse you will need to note the version, and then you'll need to add that copyright clause to the copyright page.

Some publishers follow the Bible guidelines in the *Chicago Manual of Style*, others follow *The Christian Writer's Manual of Style* (the newest version at this writing was updated in 2016). However,

I've found that most Christian publishers have their own style guides for how to abbreviate Bible book names (Deut., or Deu., or Dt.), how to write references (hyphen, comma or en-dash between verse spans), and the capitalizations of various scriptural words (temple or Temple; rapture or Rapture). Some publishers use the lowercase letters *a* or *b* to indicate in the reference that the author is using the first or second part of a verse (Psalm 139:14a); others don't do that. If you are under contract to a publisher, ask for their style guide to help you prepare your manuscript. If not, make your decisions at this point and note them on your style sheet so that you'll be consistent.

Over the years, I've gathered up a list of items important to remember when quoting from or otherwise using Scripture in your writing. Following are my ten key rules for quoting and sourcing Scripture.

(1) Know what version(s) you're using—and quote it correctly.

"Be careful, for writing books is endless" (Ecclesiastes 12:12 NLT).

"Of making many books there is no end" (Ecclesiastes 12:12 NIV).

"There's no end to the publishing of books" (Ecclesiastes 12:12 MSG).

Follow the various style guides or the style guide from the publisher for the details; barring that, be consistent. Use your style sheet to make note of how you write the references (1:3, 4 or 1:3-4 or 1:3–4) and whether you're writing Bible book names out in full or abbreviating them (and how you abbreviate them). The moral of the story is, be consistent. Consistency will keep your pages looking tidy.

By far the most important key to quoting Scripture is to *quote* it accurately. I can't stress enough: *Be careful as you type the verses.* If I had a nickel for every time I've seen typos in quoted verses ... well, I'd have a lot of nickels. And if you're copying over from Bible Gateway or some other electronic Bible, still double check yourself. Do a comparison read after you're finished, a phrase at a time—read aloud and read the punctuation as well from the original and to your transcription. If you're working with an electronic Bible, minimize both screens so that you can see your document and see the electronic page at the same time. That makes it much easier than trying to flip back and forth between screens.

While We're Talking About Quoting

While I make special note in this chapter focusing on quoting Bible text, understand that *anything* you quote should be handled with just as much care. Whether it's a religious text, classic literature, a book, a magazine or newspaper article, or words from someone's blog, be sure that you quote exactly.

In addition, just as you would be careful of context in quoting from Scripture, you want to be careful of context when quoting from any other source. Be sure to read thoroughly so that you don't misrepresent anything that you quote or misrepresent the author.

(2) Be sure that "LORD" or "GOD" is small caps where appropriate.

Throughout the Old Testament (and in the New Testament when it's quoting the Old), the word Lord will often be rendered as LORD, with the "ord" as small caps (and in a few cases, GOD is that way as well, but not often). When you see LORD in small caps, you're seeing the translators using this special formatting to show that the word is the Hebrew word for the name of God, YHWH or Yahweh. It is important that when you quote Bible verses that have this small caps, you include those small caps.

> For the LORD is good and his love endures forever; his faithfulness continues through all generations. (Psalm 100:5 NIV)

Quickly do small capitals by highlighting the "ord" (make sure that you start with the letters in lower case) and then pressing Control

+ Shift + K. You can also highlight the three letters, navigate to the Home ribbon, Font tab with the dropdown to open up the Font menu, and then click on the box for "Small caps." Mac users, do Command + Shift + K.

(3) Don't worry about italics.

Some Old Testament texts italicize words not technically in their source texts. You may not see these on electronic Bibles, but if you're copying from your Bible, you may see various words italicized. Unless the words are italicized for other purposes (for example, in the New Testament where Jesus is speaking in Aramaic), then don't worry about copying so exactly that you also copy the italics. Most publisher style guides specify not to do that.

For example, Genesis 1:10 in the King James Version reads, "And God called the dry *land* Earth; and the gathering together of the waters called the Seas: and God saw that *it was* good." Notice the italics on "land" and "it was." When you copy this verse into your manuscript, you don't need to italicize those words. (Note that you *do* need to maintain the capital letters beginning Earth and Seas.)

However, if you're quoting Jesus as here in Matthew 27:46 in the New International Version (2011): "About three in the afternoon Jesus cried out in a loud voice, '*Eli, Eli, lema sabachthani?*' (which means 'My God, my God, why have you forsaken me?')," then preserve the italics because this verse is following the rule of putting foreign language words in italics.

(4) Use quotation marks accurately.

Generally, when you're going to quote a verse, you will put it in quotation marks, as here, "But God showed his great love for us by sending Christ to die for us while we were still sinners" (Romans 5:8 NLT). However, if you're quoting a passage with more than five lines, generally you'll put that in a block, so then you will not use open and close quotes (this line-count rule applies to quoting any kind of block text—not only Scripture). For example:

> We can rejoice, too, when we run into problems
> and trials, for we know that they help us develop
> endurance. And endurance develops strength of
> character, and character strengthens our confident
> hope of salvation. And this hope will not lead to
> disappointment. For we know how dearly God loves
> us, because he has given us the Holy Spirit to fill our
> hearts with his love. When we were utterly helpless,
> Christ came at just the right time and died for us
> sinners. (Romans 5:3–6 NLT)

If you're running a quoted Scripture verse into your text that has a quote within it, you will need to change the double quotes to single quotes, such as, "Jesus told him, 'I am the way, the truth, and the life'" (John 14:6 NLT). Notice that since I had to enclose the quote in quotation marks to quote it here in this paragraph, I needed to change the original double quotation marks around Jesus' words to single quotation marks. Also, if you need to capitalize a letter at the beginning or lower case a letter because you're folding the quote into a sentence you wrote, do so.

The exception is when you do a block (as above). Since there are no open or close quotes around a block of text, any internal quotation marks will remain as in the original.

(5) Don't include verse numbers.

When you're quoting more than one verse, either running into your text or in a block quote, you don't need to include the verse numbers at each verse. These verse numbers may carry over from electronic Bible software if you copy a block of material, so be sure to remove them.

"Versification" refers to those Bibles where each verse starts in a new paragraph; that is, the verses are not run together to create paragraphs. When you're copying from such Bibles, you do not need to keep the verses separate. That is simply a stylistic decision made by the Bible publisher. For your purposes when quoting, run the material together into one paragraph.

The same rule applies to quoting poetry in Scripture. Type the poetry into paragraph form. For example, Psalm 139:13–14 in NLT looks like this in the Bible text:

You made all the delicate, inner parts of my body
and knit me together in my mother's womb.
Thank you for making me so wonderfully complex!
Your workmanship is marvelous—how well I know it.

If you don't want to format it like poetry, you may put it into a paragraph. "You made all the delicate, inner parts of my body and knit me together in my mother's womb. Thank you for making me so wonderfully complex! Your workmanship is marvelous—how well I know it" (Psalm 139:13–14 NLT).

If you want to use a block quote, render it with the poetry lines indented correctly, or, if you had enough more verses to require a block, do it this way for Psalm 139:13-18 in the NLT:

> You made all the delicate, inner parts of my body and knit me together in my mother's womb. Thank you for making me so wonderfully complex! Your workmanship is marvelous—how well I know it. You watched me as I was being formed in utter seclusion, as I was woven together in the dark of the womb. You saw me before I was born. Every day of my life was recorded in your book. Every moment was laid out before a single day had passed. How precious are your thoughts about me, O God. They cannot be numbered! I can't even count them; they outnumber the grains of sand! And when I wake up, you are still with me!

Also note that when presenting poetry together into paragraph lines, you may need to lowercase some letters. The text may have capital letters at the beginning of each new line or verse, but when run together, these would be incorrect. Fix the capitalization to match sentence case.

(6) Watch your punctuation.

In addition to the quotation marks, above, watch for other types of punctuation. The style for typing a verse within the text of a manuscript is generally quotation followed by punctuation. Notice in the following example that there is no punctuation at the end of the verse itself; instead, the period follows the close parenthesis of the reference.

"In the beginning the Word already existed" (John 1:1 NLT).

If your verse ends in a question mark or exclamation point, put that inside the close quote and put a period after the close parenthesis.

"Who has a claim against me that I must pay?" (Job 41:11 NIV).

"And Abraham said to God, 'If only Ishmael might live under your blessing!'" (Genesis 17:18 NIV).

Notice in the Genesis verse that I had to add the open and close quotation marks around the entire verse, which means I had to put single quotations marks around Abraham's words. The exclamation point stays, and the period is placed after the close parenthesis.

However, note that when you have a text in a block, the punctuation closes out the block with the reference *without* punctuation following.

> You saw me before I was born. Every day of my life was recorded in your book. Every moment was laid out before a single day had passed. How precious are your thoughts about me, O God. They cannot be numbered! I can't even count them; they outnumber the grains of sand! And when I wake up, you are still with me! (Psalm 139:16–18 NLT)

(7) Watch how you use ellipses.

Most publishers are fine with quoting a portion of a verse without ellipses at the beginning or the end. That is, if you're talking about

Jesus and what he said, and you want to drop off the "Jesus said" at the beginning of the verse and just quote what he said, you don't need to include ellipses to indicate that you dropped the words "Jesus said." The same often goes if you're quoting just the first part and not the end; you don't necessarily have to include the ellipses trailing at the end. Of course, you must use ellipses if you're dropping material from the middle of the verse, or dropping a verse from a series of verses, to indicate that material is missing.

However, I would advise you to make these kind of changes carefully. Always remember that you're working with God's Word. Be respectful of it for its own sake and for the sake of your readers. Be careful not to cause contextual problems with ellipses. Make sure that you are letting the verse say what it says, without causing confusion by dropping out parts of it.

(8) Follow consistency in references.

While it's important to know what to do with the Bible book name throughout your references, you will need to make several other consistency decisions as well—or you might ask your publisher how they want you to do it. (You can also get advice from *The Christian Writer's Manual of Style*.) This attention to consistency may seem like overkill, but trust me, if you make these decisions early on and are consistent, your manuscript will make so much more sense to an editor and ultimately to your readers. For instance, in the *Christian Writer's Manual of Style*, you'll find an alphabetized text that includes extensive word lists of Christian terms and suggested spellings and capitalizations, along with every other question you might have and want to look up (for example, "Clerical titles and clerical positions" and how to use them is in the section for the letter C).

If you're going to be quoting several verses from the same chapter (say, you're discussing the story of Daniel in the lions' den and your readers know you're in Daniel 6, but throughout the coming pages you're working your way through different verses), decide how to handle each reference. It might look awkward to put the full book name or even the abbreviated book name and chapter in each reference after each quote. Maybe opt for saying (verse 6) and (verse 7) and (verses 8–9), or maybe even (v. 6) and (v. 7) and (vv. 8–9). Or maybe keep just the chapter without the book name (6:6), (6:7), (6:8–9). The most important consideration is clarity for your readers.

(9) Let readers know if you are using emphasis.

Perhaps you want to emphasize a portion of a verse you're quoting. Do that by putting it in italics, but let your readers know that the emphasis is yours. (This rule is true for quoting from anything anywhere, not just Scripture.) After the reference, say something like "italics mine" or "emphasis mine." If you want to focus on the word *patience* in these verses about the fruit of the Spirit, do this: "But the Holy Spirit produces this kind of fruit in our lives: love, joy, peace, *patience*, kindness, goodness, faithfulness, gentleness, and self-control" (Galatians 5:22–23 NLT, emphasis mine).

(10) Use brackets to indicate added material.

As we've established, quoting from anywhere is sacrosanct. Leave the quote exactly as it is rendered—and this rule is obviously extremely important in Scripture. But sometimes, you're quoting and must give your readers some context. Indicate that you are editing the direct quote by putting the edited material in brackets.

For example, quoting Genesis 45:25, "So they went up out of Egypt and came to their father Jacob in the land of Canaan" (NIV). You might need to explain who "they" refers to. Revise the verse to explain who "they" is by replacing the word and putting the referent in brackets, as follows: "So [Joseph's brothers] went up out of Egypt and came to their father Jacob in the land of Canaan."

Don't use parentheses, because parentheses could be part of the quote. The brackets make it clear that you have added the material.

One Last Word

I've read a few devotionals that obviously took a verse out of context. I've read material from people who didn't know Scripture, so wrote that King David led the Israelites out of Egypt, or that the Bible has sixty-six chapters. Sometimes writers didn't understand the difference between the Old Testament Joseph and the New Testament

Joseph, or the Old Testament Saul and the New Testament Saul. (I once had someone who clearly didn't know Scripture do an index for me—and all the Sauls and Josephs were together in one spot, clearly not differentiated. What a mess.)

With Scripture, follow three Cs: watch *context*, take *care*, be *correct*.

When you quote a verse, check the *context*. Understand, for example, that the words of Job's friends in the book of Job often misrepresent God's truth. Understand that the proverbs are not promises but general principles. Read the verses surrounding any verse you desire to quote. Know that Scripture never contradicts itself; look at any verse within its immediate context and in the context of Scripture as a whole.

Take *care* to correctly handle the word of truth. Don't make Scripture say what it doesn't say. Don't use ellipses to remove "inconvenient" material. Scripture is pretty clear about many issues that seem to be up for debate among Christians, and between Christians and the world. Do as the Berean Jews who didn't just agree with everything the apostle Paul said when he preached; instead, "they received the message with great eagerness and examined the Scriptures every day to see if what Paul said was true" (Acts 17:11 NIV).

Finally, be *correct* in your quotations, your verse references. Many times I've copyedited material where the author is talking about Elisha but his quotations are consistently from 1 Kings. I know that most of Elijah's story is in 1 Kings; Elisha's is in 2 Kings. A cross check of his references revealed that he simply had put the incorrect book title. It's easy to make mistakes, but double check every quotation and every reference.

Know Scripture, know the context of every verse you read, and carefully reread everything even if you think you know the story. I say that because I recall one time writing a devotional about Zacchaeus. Everyone knows that story, right? I just wrote it from memory because, good grief, how many times have I read it? I created a wonderful (I thought) scene with Zacchaeus up in the tree waiting—having climbed the tree several minutes ahead of time in anticipation of Jesus' arrival. I then focused on what Zacchaeus was thinking as he waited. I was proud of myself, and then I went back to the Bible text to read the story. The text clearly says that *because he could not see over the crowd,*

Zacchaeus *ran ahead of the crowd* and climbed the tree. So he hadn't planned ahead and waited in the tree; he had to run ahead. Thus, I had to go back and revise my lovely scene in order to make it true to Scripture.

When you're working with Scripture, it is vital to be marinating in Scripture in order to "correctly handle the word of truth." What I mean by that phrase is that you need to be reading the Bible every day, studying it, hearing it, and, of course, living it.

Conclusion

Congratulations again on completing the first draft. I hope I've given you the tools to do the next step—to self-edit your manuscript and polish it until it shines.

I know, I gave you a lot of information here. Don't worry about trying to remember everything; instead, use this book as a resource. Come back when you're ready to format your manuscript and follow the guidelines. Stop in again when you need a reminder about comma usage. Visit my website for further technical advice. Write me with questions if you get stuck at linda@lindaktaylor.com or use the form on my website.

It's all about the words. Here's to yours getting into the world!

About the Author

Linda Taylor has been working in writing, editing, and publishing since she graduated from Houghton College in upstate New York in 1980. She's been fortunate to be able to have a long career doing a job she loves.
Linda grew up in a military family and spent her four high school years in Bonn, Germany, where her dad worked with the American Embassy. After college, she moved to Wheaton, Illinois, to work at the Evangelical Teacher Training Association (now ETA) editing their teaching materials.

She married Tom in 1983 and began working in the national office of Youth for Christ. There, she got involved writing and editing notes and features with the team from YFC and Tyndale House Publishers that created *The Life Application Study Bible.* This study Bible has gone on to be one of the best-selling study Bibles of all time. Out of that project grew a company called Livingstone (now Barton-Veerman Company), a book packager dedicated to helping publishers create great books and Bibles. Linda has worked with them for three decades.

The family relocated to the cornfields of Indiana and a small town (with annual tractor parades!) where Linda now is an instructor in the Communication department teaching courses in the Professional Writing major at Taylor University in Upland, Indiana.

Linda received her MA in English from Ball State University in Muncie, Indiana, and her MFA in Creative Writing from Ashland University in Ohio. She enjoys speaking at writers conferences around the country and continuing to freelance because … well … it's all about the words.

Linda and Tom have three children and five grandchildren.

Follow Linda K. Taylor

Email: linda@lindaktaylor.com

Website: lindaktaylor.com

Twitter: @lindaedits

Instagram: lindataylor5558

Endnotes

[1]Kent Hall, "Why We All Need a Developmental Editor," www.blurb.com, Dec 18, 2014. Retrieved Oct 6, 2016 from http://www.blurb.com/blog/why-we-all-need-a-developmental-editor/?utm_source=facebookr&utm_medium=social&utm_campaign=all_blogaware.

[2] William Haywood Henderson, "Toward a 'Final' Draft," instructor notes for Ashland University from a lecture given on July 19, 2016.

[3] Ibid.

[4] Harper Lee, *Go Set a Watchman* (New York: HarperCollins, 2015), 6.

[5] Ibid., 10.

[6] Ibid., 114.

[7] Harper Lee, *To Kill a Mockingbird* (New York: Warner Books, 1960), 46.

[8] Ibid., 5.

[9] "Harper Lee to Publish 'To Kill a Mockingbird' Sequel, Decades Later," 3 Feb 2015, mashable.com/2015/02/03/harper-lee-go-set-a-watchman/#FTQqW_ewwiqd. Accessed 5 Feb 2017.

[10] A. Scott Berg, *Maxwell Perkins: Editor of Genius* (New York: E. P. Dutton, 1978), 15-16.

[11] Berg, 64.

[12] Matthew J. Bruccoli, ed. *The Sons of Maxwell Perkins: Letters of F. Scott Fitzgerald, Ernest Hemingway, Thomas Wolfe, and Their Editor* (Columbia, SC: University of South Carolina Press, 2004), 28.

[13] F. Scott Fitzgerald, *The Great Gatsby* (New York: Simon & Schuster, 2003), 127.

[14] Kirsten Reach, "Ten Nights on Long Island: The Great Gatsby's Early Reviews," mphbooks.com, May 9, 2013. Retrieved January 24, 2017 from https://www.mhpbooks.com/ten-nights-on-long-island-the-great-gatsbys-early-reviews/.

[15] Thanks to Andy Scheer. For more information, see http://andyscheer.com.

[16] Linda K. Taylor, comment on "So I'm Writing a Book," Linda Taylor (blog), Oct 21, 2016, comment posted Oct 21, 2016 (8:32 p.m.) at http:/lindaktaylor.com.

[17] "Avoiding 'Christianeze' in Your Writing," Evangelical Press Association, www.evangelicalpress.com. Retrieved Nov 6, 2016 from http://www.evangelicalpress.com/christianese-2/.

[18] Luke Cawley, "How NOT to Speak Christianese," InterVarsity. org, October 1, 2012. Retrieved November 6, 2016 from http://evangelism.intervarsity.org/how/conversation/how-not-speak-christianese

Resources

Books about Grammar and Editing

Associated Press. *The Associated Press Stylebook 2015 and Briefing on Media Law.* New York: Basic Books, 2015.

Bell, James Scott. *Revision and Self-editing for Publication: Techniques for Transforming Your First Draft into a Novel that Sells.* Cincinnati, OH: Writer's Digest Books, 2012.

Bell, Susan. *The Artful Edit: On the Practice of Editing Yourself.* New York: W. W. Norton & Company, 2007.

Berg, A. Scott. *Maxwell Perkins: Editor of Genius.* New York: E. P. Dutton, 1978.

Browne, Renni, and Dave King, *Self-Editing for Fiction Writers: How to Edit Yourself into Print.* New York: Harper, 2004.

Bruccoli, Matthew J., ed. *The Sons of Maxwell Perkins: Letters of F. Scott Fitzgerald, Ernest Hemingway, Thomas Wolfe, and Their Editor.* Columbia, SC: University of South Carolina Press, 2004.

Chicago Manual of Style, 16th ed. Chicago: University of Chicago Press, 2010.

Dunham, Steve. *The Editor's Companion: An Indispensable Guide to Editing Books, Magazines, Online Publications, and More.* Cincinnati, OH: Writer's Digest Books, 2014.

Einsohn, Amy. *The Copyeditor's Handbook: A Guide for Book Publishing and Corporate Communications.* Oakland, CA: University of California Press, 2011.

Gerke, Jeff. *The First 50 Pages: Engage Agents, Editors and Readers and Set up Your Novel for Success.* Cincinnati, Ohio: F+W Media, 2011.

Gilad, Suzanne. *Copyediting & Proofreading for Dummies*. New York: Wiley Publishing, Inc., 2007.

Gookin, Dan. *Word 2016 for Dummies*. New York: W. W. Norton & Company, 2015.

Gross, Gerald, ed. *Editors on Editing*. New York: Grove Press, 1993.

Hensley, Dennis, and Diana Savage. *Finding Success with Your Dream Writing Projects*. Friendswood, TX: Bold Vision Books, 2017.

Hudson, Robert. *The Christian Writer's Manual of Style*. 4th ed. Grand Rapids, MI: Zondervan, 2016.

Ide, Kathy. *Proofreading Secrets of Best-selling Authors*. Raleigh, NC: Lighthouse Publishing of the Carolinas, 2016,

King, Stephen. *On Writing*. New York: Pocket Books, 2001.

Lerner, Betsy. *The Forest for the Trees: An Editor's Advice to Writers*. New York: Riverhead Books, 2010.

McIntyre, John E. *The Old Editor Says: Maxims for Writing and Editing*. Baltimore, MD: Apprentice House, 2013.

Morrell, Jessica Page Morrell, *Thanks, But This Isn't For Us*. New York: Jeremy P. Tarcher/Penguin, 2009.

Norris, Mary. *Between You and Me: Confessions of a Comma Queen*. New York: W. W. Norton & Company, 2015.

Norton, Scott. *Developmental Editing: A Handbook for Freelancers, Authors, and Publishers*. Chicago: University of Chicago Press, 2011.

Rabiner, Susan, and Alfred Fortunato. *Thinking Like Your Editor: How to Write Great Serious Nonfiction—and Get It Published*. New York: W. W. Norton & Company, 2002.

Saller, Carol Fisher. *The Subversive Copy Editor, Second Edition: Advice from Chicago (or, How to Negotiate Good Relationships with Your Writers, Your Colleagues, and . . .* Guides to Writing, Editing, and Publishing, 2nd ed. Chicago: University of Chicago Press, 2016.

Stein, Sol. *Stein on Writing*. New York: St. Martin's Griffin, 1995.

Strunk, William, and E. B. White. *The Elements of Style*, 4th ed. New York: Pearson, 1999.

Stuart, Sally. *The Writing World Defined A–Z*. Friendswood, TX: Bold Vision Books, 2015.

Tan, Amy. *The Opposite of Fate: Memories of a Writing Life*. New York: Penguin Books, 2003.

Zinsser, William. *On Writing Well: The Classic Guide to Writing Nonfiction*, 6th ed. New York: HarperPerennial, 1998.

Websites for Editing Help

Grammar and style guides

grammarly.com

owl.english.purdue.edu/exercises/ (grammar exercises)

chompchomp.com/exercises.htm (grammar exercises)

quickanddirtytips.com/grammar-girl

www.bartleby.com/141/ (*Elements of Style*)

owl.english.purdue.edu/owl/ (search for various style options)

chicagomanualofstyle.org (*Chicago Manual of Style* online—paid subscription)

Copyright law

www.copyright.gov/title17/

janefriedman.com/2013/07/15/the-fair-use-doctrine/

Some blogs to follow

lindaktaylor.com

americaneditor.wordpress.com

booksandsuch.com/blog

dochensley.com

jerryjenkins.com

rachellegardner.com

stevelaube.com/blog

theeditorsblog.net

Some Christian Publishing Websites

amgpublishers.com (AMG)

augsburgfortress.org (Augsburg Fortress)

bakerpublishinggroup.com (Baker Publishing Group, includes Bethany House)

barbourbooks.com (Barbour)

bhpublishinggroup.com (Broadman Holman)

boldvisionbooks.com (Bold Vision Books)

crossway.org (Crossway)

davidccook.com (David C. Cook)

faithwords.com (FaithWords)

focusonthefamily.com (Focus on the Family)

hachettebookgroup.com (Hachette)

harpercollinschristian.com (Zondervan/Thomas Nelson)

harvesthousepublishers.com (Harvest House)

hendrickson.com (Hendrickson)

ivpress.com (InterVarsity)

kregel.com (Kregel)

lifeway.com (Lifeway)

moodypublishers.com (Moody)

rbc.org (Regular Baptist Press, "Daily Bread")

tyndale.com (Tyndale)

worthypublishing.com (Worthy)

Follow the Publishing Business Websites

awpwriter.org

janefriedman.com

newpages.com

publishersweekly.com

pw.org

right-writing.com

shelf-awareness.com

writersdigest.com

writerswin.com

writerunboxed.com

Made in the USA
Lexington, KY
16 September 2017